RUDOLF STEINER

ESOTERIC LESSONS FOR THE FIRST CLASS OF THE FREE SCHOOL FOR SPIRITUAL SCIENCE AT THE GOETHEANUM

Volume Three

Lessons One through Seven
(Recapitulation)

between September 6 and September 20, 1924 in Dornach
for members of the Free School for Spiritual Science

Translated by Frank Thomas Smith

ESOTERIC LESSONS FOR THE FIRST CLASS
OF THE FREE SCHOOL FOR SPIRITUAL SCIENCE AT THE GOETHEANUM

Translated by
Frank Thomas Smith

Cover designed by
James D. Stewart

Rudolf Steiner Portrait by
Peter Gospodinov

Initial "M" designed by
Rudolf Steiner

For researching these lectures on-line, see GA 241a and GA270:
https://wn.elib.com/Lectures/GA241a/English/eLib2016/FstCl3_index.html
https://wn.elib.com/Lectures/GA270/English/eLib2018a/FstCs3_index.html

Anthroposophical Publications
Visit the website at:
https://anthroposophicalpublications.org/

Printed in the United States of America

ISBN: 978-1-948302-32-6 hard
978-1-948302-33-3 paper
978-1-948302-34-0 eBook

First Printing: April 2022
Anthroposophical Publications

Contents

INTRODUCTION

During the re-founding of the Anthroposophical Society at Christmas 1923, Rudolf Steiner also reconstituted the "Esoteric School" which had originally functioned in Germany from 1904 until 1914, when the outset of the First World War made its continuance impossible.

However, the original school was only for a relatively few selected individuals, whereas the new school was incorporated into the *School for Spiritual Science* at the Goetheanum in Dornach, Switzerland.

Rudolf Steiner was only able to give nineteen lessons — plus seven "recapitulation" lessons — for the First Class before his illness and death. His intention had been to develop three classes. After his death, the Anthroposophical Society's Executive Council was faced with the dilemma of what to do about the Esoteric School — to try to continue it without Rudolf Steiner, or not. He had not designated a successor. And what to do with the stenographic records of the Class lectures.

Rudolf Steiner had always insisted that the lectures were not to be published. In fact, the members of the School were only permitted to copy the mantra — and not the text of the lectures - for their own personal contemplation. The dilemma was further complicated by the dispute between Marie Steiner — Rudolf Steiner's legal heir — and the rest of the Executive council, which claimed **all** of Steiner's lectures for the Society. (The dispute was eventually settled by the Swiss courts in favor of Mrs. Steiner.)

The Anthroposophical Society was permitted to hand out manuscripts of the lectures to its so-called designated "readers", who read each lecture to the members of the school in their particular area or country. This system is still practiced.

Marie Steiner wrote:

"How can we preserve the treasure with which we have been entrusted? Not by hiding it away, thereby simply giving our enemies the opportunity to do with it what they will, but by trusting in the good spiritual powers and thereby giving new generations the possibility of receiving a stimulus in their souls that will kindle the spiritual light slumbering there, a light that will awaken in their souls what the powers of destiny have sown in them."

Marie Steiner, letter of January 4, 1948

The lectures were published in German in manuscript book form in 1977 by the Rudolf Steiner Estate (Nachlassverwaltung — Marie Steiner's legal successor) in a limited edition and sold only upon written request to anthroposophists.

However, pirated editions containing errors and falsifications occurred to the extent that the Rudolf Steiner Estate decided to make the printed volumes in German generally available in 1992.

As far as we know, the lectures in English translation are appearing in public availability for the first time in Southern Cross Review.

Frank Thomas Smith — Editor

LESSON ONE
(Recapitulation)

Dornach, September 6, 1924

My dear friends,

As it turns out, many more friends have come to this Class Lesson — and probably will to the next lessons as well — who had not attended the previous ones. So, it would be impossible to simply continue in the same way as we have with the previous lessons. But it is also true that a repetition of these Class Lessons will not be a disadvantage for those members of this esoteric school who participated in the earlier lessons, because the content of this esoteric school is such that it works again and again on the soul. Therefore, for those who today are experiencing a repetition, it also constitutes a continuation.

But for all those who are here for the first time it means something else: it means an acquaintance with the beginning of the esoteric path.

And even those who are far advanced on the esoteric path see in it the advantages of their continued striving, in that again and again they return to the beginning. This return to the beginning is always also the endeavor to reach a more advanced stage. We should therefore consider this lesson of today in that sense. And so for the members of the School who are here for the first time, the meaning of the School must be explained beforehand.

As the impulse of the Christmas Conference with the spiritual laying of the foundation stone of the Anthroposophical Society took place in this hall, from now on an esoteric breath is to flow through the whole Anthroposophical Society — as I said yesterday — an esoteric breath that can already be noted in everything undertaken within the Anthroposophical Society since Christmas. The nucleus of this esoteric activity of the Anthroposophical Society must be the Esoteric School. This Esoteric School, coming from the entire character of anthroposophy, is to take the place of what has been previously attempted as the so-called Free School for Spiritual Science, which cannot exactly be described as having been successful.

It was at the time when I did not yet personally have the leadership of the Anthroposophical Society, and thus had to entrust those who wanted to try something, to let them try. In the future, this cannot continue. The intention of what was formed together with me as the Christmas impulse was that the Free School for Spiritual Science, with its various sections, would form an esoteric nucleus for all the esoteric work in the Anthroposophical Society.

An esoteric school, however, is not founded as an earthly entity. An esoteric school can only be one if it is the earthly reflection of what has been founded in the supersensible worlds. And it has often been declared among anthroposophists that in the succession of the reigning hierarchy of Archangels, those who reign over human spiritual life, the Archangel Michael took over this guidance during the last third of the nineteenth century. And it was made known that this guidance has a very special significance for the spiritual life and evolution of humanity on earth.

It is the case that in human evolution life is guided successively by seven Archangels who together comprise the spiritual ruling substance of the planetary system, to which the sun, earth and moon also belong. The impulse of one of these Archangels lasts about three to four centuries. And when we consider the Archangel under whose impulse the spiritual life of the present stands, when we consider Michael, we have the Archangelos who possesses the spiritual force of the sun in everything he does and supports.

Previously, again lasting for three to four centuries — that is, from the last third of the nineteenth century back through three to four centuries — was the reign of the Archangelos Gabriel, who mostly bears the moon's forces in his impulses.

And going further back we come to the centuries in which a kind of revolution against spiritual activity and spiritual being in humanity took place during the middle ages, even by those who were the bearers of civilization — the reign of Samuel, who had his impulses in the Mars forces.

When we go even further back we come to the era in which a medicinally oriented alchemy deeply influenced spiritual life under the rule of the Archangelos Gabriel, who bears the Mercury forces in his impulses.

And when we go even further back, we are approaching more and more the Mystery of Golgotha, but have not yet reached it. We find there the reign of Zachariel, who bears the Jupiter forces in his impulses, and the reign of Anael — with whom we are getting very close to the Mystery of Golgotha — who bears the Venus forces in his impulses. Then we come to the time when the brilliance of the Mystery of Golgotha asserted itself against a profound spiritual darkness on earth — under the reign of Oriphiel, who bears the Saturn forces in his impulses.

Then we come back to the previous reign of Michael, that coincides with the great international, cosmopolitan impulses through Alexander the Great and Aristotle, which until that point was brought to humanity by means of the Greek mysteries and spirituality, and was then brought by Alexander over to Asia, to North Africa, so that what was the spiritual life of a small territory streamed out to the whole civilized world of those times. For it is always an attribute of a Michael era that what had previously blossomed in one place streams out to other localities in a cosmopolitan manner.

Thus, after having completed the cycle of successive Archangeloi epochs, we always return to the same Archangelos. We can go back further — again through the succession of Gabriel, Samuel, Raphael, Zachariel, Anael, Oriphiel — and would come again to Michael. And we would find that after the Michael era streams over us, an Oriphiel era follows.

So, my dear friends, we should be aware that the Michael impulse lives in the way characterized in everything which is spiritual activity and being in the present. But it is a more important Michael era than the previous ones. I would like to emphasize this.

When the Anthroposophical Society was placed at the service of the esoteric during the Christmas Conference, its esoteric nucleus, this Esoteric School, could only be founded by the spiritual power which is incumbent for its guidance at this time. Thus, we are in this Esoteric School as one which the spirit of the times himself, Michael, has founded; for it is the Michael-School of the present.

And only then, my dear friends, can you correctly understand what is being said here — when you are aware that nothing else is being said but what the Michael stream itself wishes to bring to humanity in the present time. All the words which will be spoken in this School are Michael words. Michael will is all that is willed in this School. You are all students of Michael in that you are present in the right way in this School. Only then, when you are aware of this, is it possible to be present in this School in the right way — with the correct disposition and attitude, feeling yourselves to be members not only of what enters the world as an earthly institution, but as a heavenly institution.

It is of course therefore a condition that every member of this School accept certain self-evident responsibilities. It is a property of the Christmas impulse of the Anthroposophical Society, that it has taken on the characteristic of complete openness. Therefore, nothing is demanded of members of the Anthroposophical Society other than what they themselves demand: that they receive through the Anthroposophical Society what flows within the anthroposophical spiritual movement. One does not take on further responsibilities when one becomes an anthroposophist. The responsibility for being a decent person is taken for granted.

It is otherwise when one seeks to enter this School. Then, based on the truly occult spirit of this School, the member assumes the responsibility of being a worthy representative of anthroposophy before the world with all his thinking, feeling and willing. One cannot otherwise be a member of this School.

That this is taken seriously, my dear friends, can be seen by that fact that since the short existence of this School in twenty instances temporary expulsions have already taken place. This strict measure will have to continue to be followed in the same way. One cannot play around with true esoteric matters; they must be realized with utmost earnestness. In this way, through this School the earnestness that is absolutely necessary for the anthroposophical movement to spiritually prosper can stream into it. That is what I wanted to say as an introduction.

*

If you — I'm speaking now to those of you who are here for the first time — if you receive the words spoken here as real messages from the spiritual world, as truly Michael-words, then you will be here in the right way, in the only way you should be here.

And so now we want to bring to our souls the words which resound to the human being when he objectively observes everything in the world that surrounds him — in the world above, in the middle and below. Let us look at the mute kingdom of minerals, at the sprouting plant kingdom, at the mobile animal kingdom, at the thinking kingdom of humanity on earth; let us direct our gaze to the mountains, to the seas, to the rivers, to the effervescent springs, to the shining sun, to the gleaming moon and the sparkling stars. If the human being keeps his heart open, if he can listen with the ears of soul, the admonishment resounds to him which is contained in the words which I shall now speak:

O man, know thyself!
So resounds the Cosmic-Word.
You hear it strong in soul,
You feel it firm in spirit.

Who speaks with such cosmic might?
Who speaks with such depth of heart?

Does it work through distant radiant space
Into your senses' sense of being?
Does it ring through weaving waves of time
Into your life's evolving stream?

It's you yourself who,
In feeling space, in experiencing time,

Create the Word, feeling foreign
In the soulless void of space
Because you lose the force of thought
In time's destructive flow.

And when we let the meaning and the spirit of these words work in us, then we feel the desire to go into the springs from which our true humanity flows. To really understand these words means to crave the path that leads to those waters from which the human soul flows — to seek the source of human life.

In seeking, my dear sisters and brothers, you will be rewarded to the extent it lies in your karma. But the first step will be to understand the inner meaning of the esoteric path. This esoteric path will be described in Michael-words here in this School. It will be described in such a way that everyone can follow it, but not that everyone *must* follow it, rather that it be understood; for such understanding is in itself the first step. Therefore, what Michael has to say to present-day humanity will flow in mantric words. These mantric words will at the same time be words for meditation.

Again, it will depend on karma how these words for meditation work for each individual. And the first thing is to understand that from the spoken words about human self-knowledge the desire arises to direct one's attention to the sources of human existence: O man, know thyself! Yes, this desire must awaken. We must seek: Where are the sources of what lives in the human soul, what our humanity actually is?

At first, we must observe the surroundings that have been given us. We must look around at all the little things we have been given, at all the great things we have been given. We observe the mute stone, the worm in the earth, we look at all that grows and exists and lives around us in the kingdoms of nature. We look up to the powerfully glittering stars. We listen to the turbulent thunder.

It is not by being ascetic that we can solve the riddle of our own humanity; it is not by despising the earthworm, the stars glittering in space, not by despising them as outer sensible phenomena and instead seeking an abstractly chaotic path; but when we develop a feeling for the transcendence of what shines down on us from the stars, for all that enters through the senses and becomes our perception: beauty, truth, purity, transcendence, magnificence and majesty. When you can stand there as an observer of all that surrounds you — of the plants, of the stones, of the animals, of the stars, of the clouds, of the seas, of the springs, of the mountains — and can absorb their majesty and greatness and truth and beauty and radiance, then can you first say with complete intensity: Yes, great and powerful and majestic and glorious are the worms that crawl under the earth, the stars that glitter above in heaven's space. But your being, O man, is not among them. You are not in what your senses reveal to you.

And then we direct our questioning gaze, laden with riddles, to the far distance. From here on, the esoteric path will be described in imaginations. We direct our gaze to the distance. Something like a path is shown, a path that leads to a black, night-cloaked wall that reveals itself as the beginning of deepest darkness. And we stand there, surrounded by the majesty of sensory perception, marveling at the greatness and majesty and radiance of sensory perception, but not finding our own being in it, with our gaze directed to the limits of sensory perception. But black, night-cloaked darkness begins there. But something in our heart tells us: Not here, where the sun reflects its light from all that grows and moves and lives, but there, where black, night-cloaked darkness is staring at us, are the sources of our own humanity. From out of there the answer must come to the question: O man, know thyself!

Then we go, hesitating, towards the black darkness and become aware that the first being who confronts us stands where the black, night-cloaked darkness begins. Like a previously unseen cloud formation taking shape, it becomes human-like, not weighted by gravity, but human-like nevertheless. With earnest, very earnest gaze, it meets our questioning gaze. It is the Guardian of the Threshold. For between the sun-radiating surroundings of humanity and that night-cloaked darkness there is an abyss, a deep, yawning abyss. The Guardian of the Threshold stands before us on this side of the abyss. We call him this for the following reason.

Oh, every night while sleeping the human being with his I and with his astral body is in that world that with imaginative gaze now appears as black, night-cloaked darkness; but he doesn't realize it — his soul-senses have not opened. He doesn't realize that he lives and acts among spiritual beings and spiritual facts between falling asleep and awakening; were he to consciously experience without further preparation what there is to experience there: he would be crushed! The Guardian of the Threshold protects us — therefore he is the Guardian of the Threshold — protects us against crossing the abyss unprepared. We must follow his admonitions if we wish to tread the esoteric path. He encloses the human being in darkness every night. He guards the threshold so that the human being does not, when falling asleep, enter into the spiritual-occult world unprepared.

Now he stands there — if we have sufficiently internalized our hearts and delved deeply into our souls — there he is, admonishing us as to how everything is beautiful in our surroundings, but that in this beauty we cannot find our own being and that we must seek beyond the yawning abyss of existence in the realms of night-cloaked, black darkness; that we must wait until it becomes dark here in the sunlit radiant realm of sensory light and it becomes light for us there, where now there is still only darkness.

That is what the Guardian of the Threshold reveals to our souls. We are still at a certain distance from him. We look at him, and perceive his admonishing words still from a distance, which resound so:

> Where on earthly ground, color on color
> Life is manifest in creation;
> Where from earthly matter, form on form,
> The lifeless is given shape;
> Where sentient Beings, strong in will
> Warm themselves in joy of existence;
> Where you, O man, your bodily being
> Is shaped from earth and air and light.
>
> There your true being enters
> Deep, night-cloaked, cold darkness;
> You ask in the dark sweeping expanse
> No longer, who you are and were and will be.
> For your own being the day grows dimly
> To the soul's night, to spirit-darkness;
> And you turn with angst of soul
> Toward the light that from darkness streams.

That is the Guardian of the Threshold's first admonishment, the earnest admonishment that tells us that our surroundings are beautiful and grand and sublime, radiant with light, sun-filled; but that this radiant, sun-filled world is for the human being the true darkness; that we must seek there, in the darkness, that darkness becomes light, so that humanity, illuminated from out of the darkness, can approach us, so that the riddle of humanity may be solved from out the darkness. The Guardian of the Threshold continues:

And from out of the darkness comes light,
— you in image-shape revealed —
Your likeness manifesting you,
Yet also a parable of you,
Earnest spirit-words in cosmic ether
Heard by your heart, imparting strength,

The Spirit-Messenger, who alone
Can light for you the way;
Before him the fields of sense widen,
Behind him yawn the abyss-depths.

And before his dark spirit-fields,
Hard by the yawning abyss of being,
Resounds his anciently potent creative words:
Behold, I am the only gate to knowledge.

[The mantra is written on the blackboard, with the last line underlined.]

The Guardian speaks:

Where on earthly ground, color on color
Life is manifest in creation;
Where from earthly matter, form on form,
The lifeless is given shape;
Where sentient Beings, strong in will
Warm themselves in joy of existence;
Where you, O man, your bodily being
Is shaped from earth and air and light.

There your true being enters
Deep, night-cloaked, cold darkness;
You ask in the dark sweeping expanse
No longer, who you are and were and will be.
For your own being the day grows dimly
To the soul's night, to spirit-darkness;
And you turn with angst of soul
Toward the light that from darkness streams.

And from out of the darkness comes light,

(The continuation of this phrase follows after a few lines. What comes now is an intermediate clause.)

— you in image-shape revealed,
Your likeness manifesting you,
Yet also a parable of you,
Earnest spirit-words in cosmic ether
Heard by your heart, imparting strength —

(The intermediate clause has ended; the phrase "And from the darkness comes light" continues.)

The Spirit-Messenger,
(the Guardian of the Threshold) *who alone*
Can light for you the way;
Before him the fields of sense widen,
Behind him yawn the abyss-depths.

And before his dark spirit-fields,
Hard by the yawning abyss of being,
Resounds his anciently potent creative words:
Behold, I am the only gate to knowledge.

For it is the Guardian himself who, once he has imparted to us this first admonition: to feel light as darkness, darkness as light, indicates the feelings and sensations which can come anciently potent from our souls. He speaks them aloud, does the Guardian, as his gaze becomes even more earnest, as he stretches out his arm and hand to us, he speaks further with these words:

From the distant beings in space
Who experience existence in light,

(We feel ourselves impelled to take a few steps closer to the Guardian.)

From the stages of the course of time,
Which finds expression in creating,
From the depths of heart-felt feeling
Where in the Self the world is fathomed:

They resound in the speech of the soul,
They gleam in the spirit-thoughts,
From divine curative powers,
In the cosmic formative forces
The undulating existential words:
O you man, know thyself!

It is different if we first hear these words from sensory beings, and if we correctly understand the words which resound: “O man, know thyself!”, or if they now resound before the terrible abyss of existence from the mouth of the Guardian of the Threshold himself. The same words: two different ways to grasp them. These words are mantric, for meditation, they are words which awaken the capacity in the soul to come near to the spiritual world, if they are able to ignite the soul.

[The mantra is written on the blackboard and the title and last line are underlined.]

The Guardian at the abyss

From the distant beings in space
Who experience existence in light,
From the stages of the course of time,
Which finds expression in creating,
From the depths of heart-felt feeling
Where in the Self the world is fathomed:

They resound in the speech of the soul,
They gleam in the spirit-thoughts,
From divine curative powers,
In the cosmic formative forces
The undulating existential words:
O you man, know thyself!

While the Guardian is saying these words, we have moved close to the yawning abyss of being. It is deep. There is no hope of crossing the abyss with the feet given us by the earth. We need freedom from earthly gravity. We need the wings of spiritual life in order to cross over the abyss. By at first beckoning us to the yawning abyss of existence, the Guardian of the Threshold made us aware of how our Self, before being illuminated and purified for the spiritual world, where actually today we are everywhere surrounded by hate for the spiritual world, by mockery of the spiritual world, by cowardice and fear of the spiritual world — the Guardian makes us aware of how this, our Self, which wills and feels and thinks, is constituted today in our present evolutionary cycle in its threefold character of willing, feeling and thinking. We must first recognize this before we can become aware, in real self-knowledge, of our true Self, which is implanted in us by the gods.

All three beasts, which arise from the abyss one after the other, appear to us as seen from the viewpoint of the eternal divine force of healing: human willing, human feeling, human thinking. As they appear one after the other — willing, feeling, thinking in their true form — the Guardian explains them:

We are standing at the edge of the abyss. The Guardian speaks — the beasts rise up:

Yes, you must beware of the abyss;
Otherwise its beasts will devour
You, if you pass by me in haste.
Your cosmic age has placed them there
In you as enemies of knowledge.

Behold the first beast, the crooked back,
The bony head, the scrawny body,
His skin is all a dullish blue;
Your fear of creative spiritual being
Begat the monster in your will;
Knowledge bravery alone will overcome it.

Behold the second beast, it bares
Its teeth in a warped face, scornfully it lies,
Yellow with gray spots is its body;
Your hate of spiritual revelation
Begat this weakling in your feeling;
Your flame for knowledge must subdue him.

Behold the third beast, with cloven muzzle,
Its eye is glassy, posture slouching,
Dirty-red its form appears to you;
Your doubts in the power of spiritual light
Begat this ghost within your thinking;
Your creative knowledge must make it yield.

Only when you've defeated the three
Will wings sprout upon your soul
To fly the abyss over,
Which separates you from the knowledge fields
To which your heart desires
to consecrate itself in healing.

I will write these mantric words on the blackboard next time.

When one has heard this directly from the mouth of the Guardian, one may return, remembering, to the point of departure. There exists everything before the soul that all beings in our surroundings say, if we understand them correctly; what all beings in the most distant past already said to humanity, what all beings say to humanity in the present, and what all beings will say to the human beings of the future:

O man, know thyself!
So resounds the Cosmic-Word.
You hear it strong in soul,
You feel it firm in spirit.

Who speaks with such cosmic might?
Who speaks with such depth of heart?

Does it work through distant radiant space
Into your senses' sense of being?
Does it ring through weaving waves of time
Into your life's evolving stream?

It's you yourself who,
In feeling space, in experiencing time,

Create the Word, feeling foreign
In the soulless void of space
Because you lose the force of thought
In time's destructive flow.

These are the words of the Michael-School. When they are spoken, Michael's spirit flows in waves through the room in which they are spoken. And his sign is what confirms his presence.

*

Michael-Sign (red)

Then Michael leads us to the real Rosicrucian School, which shall reveal the secrets of humanity in the past, in the present and in the future through the Father-God, the Son-God and the Spirit-God. And then pressing the seal on the words “rosae et crucis”, the words may be pronounced:

Ex deo nascimur

In Christo morimur

Per spiritum sanctum reviviscimus

accompanied by the sign of Michael's seal, which are for the first words “Ex deo nascimur” [See note]:

secondly by the words "In Christo morimur":

thirdly by the words "Per spiritum sanctum reviviscimus":

As we say the words "Ex deo nascimur", we feel them confirmed by the seal and sign of Michael —

"Ex deo nascimur" by this sign [makes the gesture — see note]:

I esteem the Father

"In Christo morimur" by this sign:

I love the Son

"Per spiritum sanctum reviviscimus" by this sign:

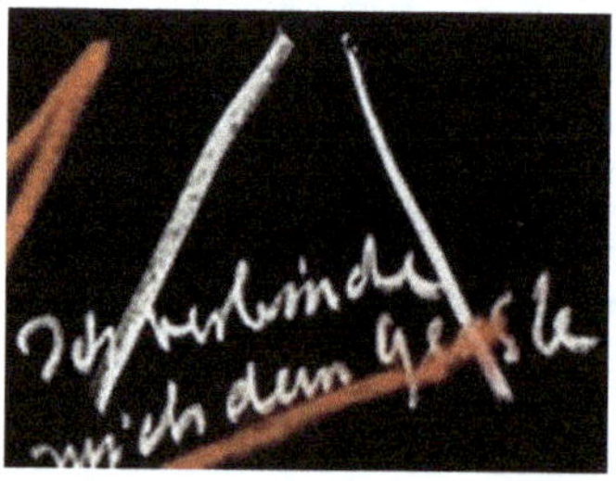

I bind myself to the Spirit

That is what the signs mean.

Michael's presence is confirmed by his seal and sign.

Michael-Sign [see note]

The mantric words written on the blackboard may only be kept by those who are legitimate members of the School, that is, who have been issued the blue certificate. No one else may possess these words. Of course, those may have them who for some reason cannot attend a particular session of the School, or because of the distance from their homes cannot attend. As members of the School they can receive them from other members.

However, in each case permission to pass on these words must be obtained. The one who is to receive the words may not request permission, but only the one who passes them on. He or she obtains permission either from Dr. Wegman or from me. This is not a mere administrative measure, but must be the basis for every passing on of the words that permission must be granted either by Dr. Wegman or by me. The words may not be sent by letters, but only personally; they may not be entrusted to the mail.

Note: It is not possible to determine from the stenographic records of the seven Repetition Lessons exactly when during each lesson, Rudolf Steiner drew the Michael-Sign and the Michael-gestures with their corresponding words, or when he made the signs and the gestures.

Lesson Two
(recapitulation)

Dornach, September 9, 1924

My dear sisters and brothers,

Despite the fact that a number of new members of this Esoteric School are present today who have not attended the previous classes, it will not be possible to repeat the introductory words. Therefore, I must insist that if the new members receive the verses from other members in the manner I will describe later, at the end of the lesson, then those who give the verses to the new members are duty bound to inform them of the conditions for membership in the School. So now we must immediately continue where we left off the last time.

*

First, however, let our souls again hear the words which resound from all the beings and events of the world to unbiased hearts and minds [Gemüte]. Everything in the following words was said to human beings in the past, is said to then in the present, and will be said to them in the future:

O man, know thyself!
So resounds the Cosmic-Word.
You hear it strong in soul,
You feel it firm in spirit.

Who speaks with such cosmic might?
Who speaks with such depth of heart?

Does it work through distant radiant space
Into your senses' sense of being?

Does it ring through weaving waves of time
Into your life's evolving stream?

It's you yourself who,
In feeling space, in experiencing time,

Create the Word, feeling foreign
In the soulless void of space

Because you lose the force of thought
In time's destructive flow.

We have seen how the person who follows these words coming to him from all the things of the world and from all the events of the world, feels the desire to leave the majestic, illustrious sensory world and enter into the world beyond the yawning abyss of being, which at first confronts the human soul as black, night-cloaked darkness. But the hope exists that in order to truly solve the riddle of humanity, what shines and is radiant in earthly life must become dark in order for the light which is in that other world, in which one's own self finds its being, comes from what appears at first as black, night-cloaked cosmic darkness.

And we have seen as we approached the path leading there in thought and feeling, the figure of the Guardian of the Threshold luminously emerged as though from a spiritual cloud-like form. We heard him speaking: for everything spoken here resounds from spiritual worlds on behalf of Michael, the leader of humanity's spiritual path in our times. For this School is the true Michael School. And he also spoke about human self-knowledge. But then he used words which at first are dismaying for the soul.

The Guardian calls us to stand close to him. He looks at us with earnest countenance. And he shows us how our willing, our feeling, our thinking appear before the countenance of the gods as imaginations. There this willing, this feeling, this thinking is not yet human; it is still animal-like. There the self-knowledge is dismaying, even shattering.

But we must pass through knowledge of that self, which is the result of the errors embedded in us by our times, our cosmic time, in order to press forward to true self-knowledge.

This erroneous self-knowledge, the knowledge of the self which we carry within us from the spirit of our times, is shown to us by the Guardian by letting the first of the beasts, which represents willing, to arise from the yawning abyss of being. Then, raising his hand and pointing to the yawning abyss of being, he lets the second beast arise, representing feeling. Again pointing to the yawning abyss of being, he lets the third beast emerge, which represents thinking.

They arise one after the other thus:

The first beast — the true spiritual form of our willing, created by the fear of knowledge, which can only be overcome by having the courage for spiritual knowledge.

And then the second beast — born from the hate of spiritual knowledge, which at the present time is in the subconscious of the Gemüt [soul, heart or mind] of all people, which can only be overcome by the right enthusiasm for knowledge, for the right heartfelt blaze of knowledge; whereas today nonchalance and tepidity in respect of knowledge, yes, hate of knowledge due to nonchalance and tepidity is in the hearts.

And then the third beast — created in its ghostly nature by doubt about the spiritual world that today gnaws at the souls' roots, and which can only be overcome if knowledge awakens in itself the strength to create in one's own soul [Gemüt] the things of the spiritual world beyond.

And the Guardian at the yawning abyss speaks the following words after we have come quite close:

Yet you must beware of the abyss;
Otherwise its beasts will devour
You, if you pass by me in haste.
Your cosmic age has placed them there
In you as enemies of knowledge.

Behold the first beast, the crooked back,
bony head, the scrawny body,
All its skin is a dull blue;
Your fear of creative spiritual being
Begot the monster in your willing;
Your fearless knowledge alone overcomes it.

Behold the second beast, it bares its teeth,
Mockingly it lies with warped countenance,
Yellow with gray spots is its body;
Your hate of spiritual revelation
Begot this weakling in your feeling;
Your burning thirst for knowledge must subdue him.

Behold the third beast, with cloven muzzle,
Its eye is glassy, posture slouching,
Dirty-red its form appears to you;
Your doubts in the power of spiritual light
Begot this ghost within your thinking;
To creative knowledge must it yield.

Only when you have overcome all three
Will wings sprout from your soul
To carry you over the abyss
Which sunders you from the knowledge fields
To which your heart desires to reach
By consecrating itself to strive for healing.

[The mantra, with underlining's, is written on the blackboard.]

The Guardian speaks at the abyss:

Yet you must beware of the abyss;
Otherwise its beasts will devour
You, if you pass by me in haste.
Your cosmic age has placed them there
In you as enemies of knowledge.

Behold the <u>first</u> beast, the crooked back,
bony head, the scrawny body,
All its skin is dullish blue;
Your <u>fear</u> of creative spiritual being
Begot the monster in your <u>willing</u>;
Your fearless knowledge alone overcomes it.

Behold the <u>second</u> beast, it bares its teeth,
mockingly it lies with a warped countenance,
Yellow with gray spots is its body;
Your hate of spiritual revelation
Begot this weakling in your <u>feeling</u>;
Your burning thirst for knowledge must subdue him.

Behold the <u>third</u> beast, with cloven muzzle,
Its eye is glassy, posture slouching,
Dirty-red its form appears to you;
Your <u>doubts</u> in the power of spiritual light
Begot this ghost within your <u>thinking</u>;
To creative knowledge must it yield.

Only when you have overcome all three
Will wings sprout from your soul
To carry you over the abyss
Which sunders you from the knowledge fields
To which your heart desires to reach
by consecrating itself to strive for healing.

When the Guardian shows us this - the shattering picture of our own being which at first confronts us as the answer to the call "Oh man, know thyself!" —, once the Guardian has shown us this picture, he approaches us in order to give us a further clarification that can begin to support us again: a clarification about the third beast, which is interwoven with our thinking; about the second beast, which is interwoven with our feeling; about the first beast, which is interwoven with our willing. And he gives us a certain teaching in what he then says. He draws our attention to how we should feel about our earthly thinking.

My dear sisters and brothers, one feels, even exoterically, that this thinking by which we acquire the things and events of the world is something abstract, something shadowy, something unreal. What is then this thinking?

We must place what this thinking really is before our souls in pictures. We imagine ourselves in front of a corpse which has recently been abandoned by a human soul and spirit. We observe this corpse. As it is now, it can never have come into being in the world. It can be nothing of itself. It can only be the remains of a living human being, who was once within it, who must have first transfigured it. The corpse lies in the coffin. Let us keep this picture in mind.

Our psychic-spiritual life, which is our own true humanity, was living before it descended from the divine-spiritual world by means of conception and birth into a physical human earthly body. There above in the divine-spiritual world it was no shadowy, abstract thought, but a psychic-spiritual living, interweaving, creating, acting being. It was alive there. Then it descended into a human body; but it died by descending. And the thinking that we have between birth and death is the corpse of the living thinking we had before descending into earthly being.

Only, my dear sisters and brothers, when we feel our thinking this way, do we feel it esoterically in the right way and struggle upward to overcome the ghostly form of the third beast, do we ascend more and more to the purely angelic form of true thinking, the dead afterimage of which lives and pulses and interweaves and acts in our physical earthly body.

As long as we consider thinking as something living, we are not experiencing the truth; only when we consider our body as the coffin of dead thinking, and we feel it deeply, are we experiencing the truth. This is what the Guardian of the Threshold at the yawning abyss of being tells us, whose words we will then hear, words which can serve us as a mantric verse. He says it to us with special intimacy.

And when we turn from thinking and observe our feeling, then we must see and feel how normal feeling, which we believe is alive in us between birth and death, is only half alive, how it continually consumes and kills something in us, how in fact it makes us spiritually hollow. Thinking is dead, and feeling is half alive, it is basically only an image-form in us. And only when we feel that this earthly feeling is a weak, half-living reflection of the solar power that emits cosmic feeling throughout the entire cosmos as general universal love, then only do we feel correctly about feeling. This the Guardian of the Threshold tells us privately, in intimacy.

And only when we feel that our will, although it lives in us, is continually tempted and attacked by spiritual opposing powers, so that its strength does not serve the divine above, but the physical below; only when we feel these opposing powers, who wish to divert us in our will from our actual divine task and completely enmesh us in earthly existence, then we will feel how these opposing powers, by usurping our will, want to bring the future of the earth under their power. If they were able to do it, if we were not alert enough to dedicate our will to the Divine, and not to the Ahrimanic earthly powers, then the earth would become problematic for the gods to whom it has belonged from the its very beginning.

The Guardian tells us this as a clarification of the three beasts:

The third beast's glassy-eyed gaze,
It is the evil counter-image
Of thinking, that denies itself
In you and chooses death,
Forsaking the spirit-forces
Which before its earthly life
Was alive in fields of spirit.

The second beast's mocking countenance,
It is the evil counter-force of feeling,
Which hollows out your own soul
And creates an empty life in it
Instead of spirit-content which,
Before earthly existence was the soul's,
Enlightened by the sun's spirit power.

The first beast's bony spirit:
It is the evil creating power
Of will, which from your own body
Estranges your strength of soul
And devotes it to the opposing powers,
Who would steal in future time
Cosmic being from godly being.

[The mantra is written in the blackboard, with underlining.]

The Guardian speaks:

The third beast's glassy-eyed gaze,
It is the evil counter-image

— it is only an "image" —

Of thinking, that denies itself
In you and chooses death,
Forsaking the spirit-forces
Which before its earthly life
Was alive in fields of spirit.

The second beast's mocking countenance,
It is the evil counter-force of feeling,

— first is "image", the second "force" —

Which hollows out your own soul
And creates an empty life in it

Instead of spirit-content which,
Before earthly existence was the soul's,
Enlightened by the sun's spirit power.

The first beast's bony spirit:

— the escalation: "image", "force", "power" —

It is the evil creating power
Of will, which from your own body
Estranges your strength of soul
And devotes it to the opposing powers,
Who would steal in future time
Cosmic being from godly being.

And the Guardian at the abyss of being leads us ever closer to true self-knowledge, which can only be ours if light arises beyond in the black, night-cloaked darkness. Therefore in the most varied ways he shows us what he first showed us in the forms of the beasts, what he then showed us in the form as it pertains to this mantric verse, and what he now once again describes, in order that we come ever and ever closer to self-knowledge, for us to have wings to cross the abyss of being, for with human feet, with heavy human feet, that is, with the outer illusions, with maya-reality, we cannot cross.

After having given us this mantric verse in confidence, the Guardian now indicates to us how we should further feel about thinking, how we should not feel it as a being; for then we are still weaving illusions if in this thinking that we have as human beings on the earth we see anything else but seeming. Selfhood being, that is, our true, real being, hides itself in thinking, doesn't live in thinking — the Guardian says. One can do nothing else but submerge into the seeming of thinking ever more, until one reaches, by submerging deeply, ever further, into the immeasurable cosmic ether, in which one at first dissolves with the soul.

If our selfhood at least feels wavering in the world's seeming, then we should revere the leading beings of the higher hierarchies who guide us. Here we feel that we need these leading beings of the higher hierarchies.

Then the Guardian exhorts us to turn from thinking to feeling, to perceive the streaming feeling in us. Thinking is still naught but seeming. But what we feel stands at least halfway close to our being. We come deeper into our own being when we feel than when we think; but we are not yet there. We are in half of our own being when we are feeling; for feeling has something unclear in it, and it is also never firm: seeming and being are intermixed in feeling. The selfhood which we seek — selfhood in the good sense of the word is — tends towards seeming. We should now submerge into seeming, into a being that is only apparent, into a seeming that energizes itself to half a being; there cosmic forces hold us, which are not mere seeming, but halfway to being: cosmic soul forces. There we should ponder in this interweaving of our own being in weaving cosmic ether; there we should ponder the living power of our own soul, which we cannot ponder by thinking because thinking is seeming.

Then we should submerge in the will, which we feel to be the being hidden in us. We cannot grasp it. But the will acts as thrust and force: being. This will climbs up from all the seeming and creates our own being, our own true being. We should turn our lives towards it. It is filled with the power of the cosmic spirit. Our own being should grasp the cosmic creative power, which fills all space, all times, all spiritual domains, and submerge in the will.

At the edge of the abyss the Guardian speaks:

> See in yourself the weaving thoughts:
> Cosmic seeming confronts you,
> Selfhood as such hides from you;
> Plunge down beneath the seeming:
> Etheric essence flows in you;
> Selfhood being should revere the
> Guiding nature of your spirit.
>
> Perceive within the flow of feeling:
> Where seeming and being within you merge,
> Your selfhood tends towards the seeming;
> So plunge down in seeming being:
> And in you are the cosmic-psychic forces;
> The selfhood, it should then ponder
> Your own soul's powers of life.
>
> Let act in you the thrust of will:
> Which climbs up from all the seeming
> With your own self creating;
> Turn your life in full toward it:
> Filled it is with cosmic force of spirit;
> Your own self should truly grasp
> Creative cosmic power in the spirit-I.

I will write this mantra on the blackboard next time, and explain it with its characteristics.

But now let us turn again to all that has spoken to the human being in the past, to what speaks in the present, to what will be spoken in the future, what will be required of him as the most holy on his life's path: self-knowledge.

> O man, know thyself!
> So resounds the Cosmic-Word.
> You hear it strong in soul,
> You feel it firm in spirit.

Who speaks with such cosmic might?
Who speaks with such depth of heart?

Does it work through distant radiant space
Into your senses' sense of being?
Does it ring through weaving waves of time
Into your life's evolving stream?

It's you yourself who,
In feeling space, in experiencing time,

Create the Word, feeling foreign
In the soulless void of space
Because you lose the force of thought
In time's destructive flow.

The next esoteric lesson of this First Class will be next Thursday at eight o'clock.

*

I must also say that the verses, which are given as mantric meditation verses from the Guardian of the Threshold on behalf of Michael, are only for members of this School. Those who for any reason could not acquire them personally, may receive them from another member of the school who has them. However, permission must be requested in each case from either Dr. Wegman or from me. This is not merely an administrative measure, but means that everything in our anthroposophical movement must be based on reality from now on. And this statement begins with the permission as a real fact, not as a mere administrative measure. The verses may not be sent by mail. Only the person who is to give the verses to another may request permission from Dr. Wegman or from me. Not the one who is to receive them, but the one who gives. One asks someone who can give them, and that one then asks.

If anyone has written down something other than the verses themselves, then I ask them to only keep it for eight days and then burn it, in order that the content of the School, which only has meaning when the Michael stream flows through it, not get outside and thereby become ineffective. It is a fundamental occult axiom, which must be observed.

And we are in an earnest occult School, in the real School of Michaeli, and thus give what flows through this school in the Michaeli Sign: [drawn on the blackboard]

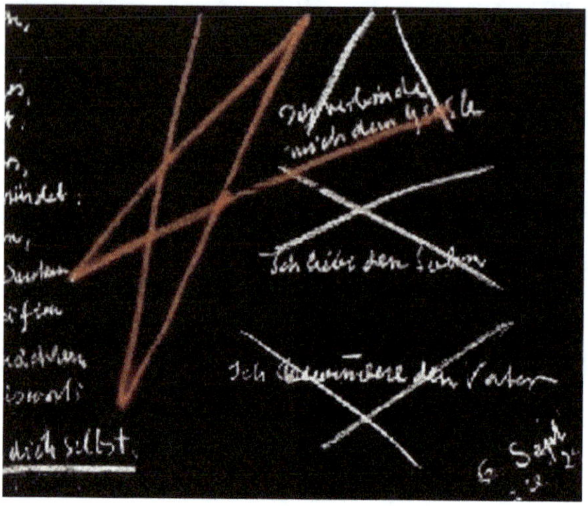

[in red]

and give it in the sense of the Rose Cross, with the symbol of the Rose Cross:

> Ex deo nascimur [the lower seal is drawn on the blackboard]
>
> In Christo Morimur [the middle seal is drawn on the blackboard]
>
> Per spiritum sanctum reviviscimus [the upper seal is drawn on the blackboard]

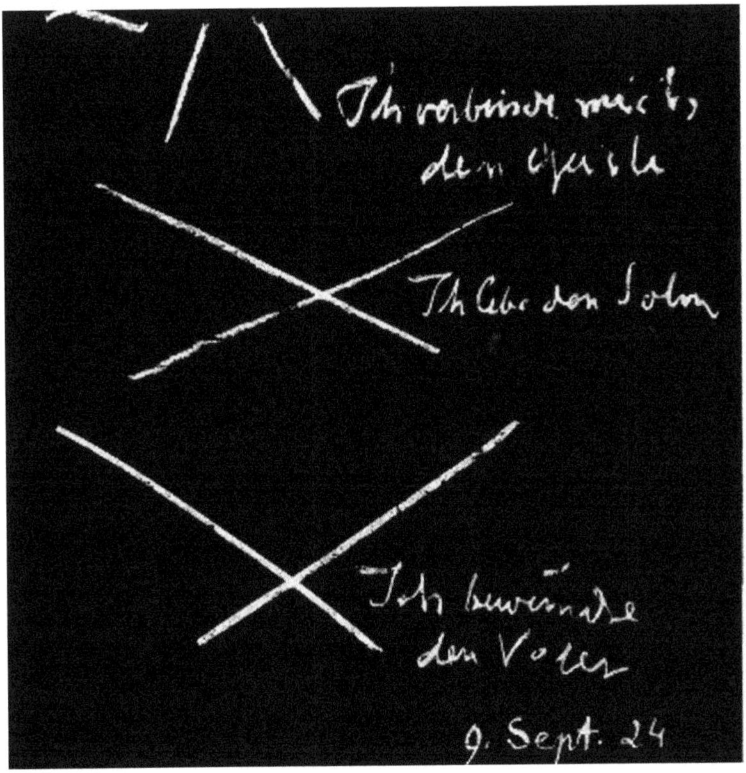

And while making this seal and sign we think of Christian Rosenkreuz:

[beside the lower seal is written:]

I revere the Father

[beside the middle seal is written:]

I love the Son

[beside the upper seal is written:]

I unite with the spirit

Per signum Michaeli:

[the michael sign — above red — is made]

[as each of the seal gestures is made, the following is spoken:]

Ex deo nascimur

In Christo morimur

Per spiritum sanctum reviviscimus

Lesson Three
(recapitulation)

Dornach, September 11, 1924

My dear sisters and brothers,

It is not possible to again give the introduction concerning the obligations for the newly participating members of the Class. I therefore request that the members who give the new ones the [mantric] verses also inform them of the conditions involved, which I will describe at the end of this lesson.

*

My dear sisters and brothers, we will again begin by letting our souls hear the words that human beings — if they have ears to hear them — can hear from all the Beings of the surrounding world, which they could hear in the past, can hear in the present and will hear in the future, which allow them to envision the need for self-knowledge — that constantly comes to them from the entire universe — which is the true bridge to what the human being needs for his thinking, for his willing, for his working in the world if he wishes to be human in the true sense of the word.

O man, know thyself!
So resounds the Cosmic-Word.
You hear it strong in soul,
You feel it firm in spirit.

Who speaks with such cosmic might?
Who speaks with such depth of heart?

Does it work through distant radiant space
Into your senses' sense of being?
Does it ring through weaving waves of time
Into your life's evolving stream?

It's you yourself who,
In feeling space, in experiencing time,

Create the Word, feeling foreign
In the soulless void of space

Because you lose the force of thought
In time's destructive flow.

*

My dear sisters and brothers, the description of the path to knowledge has led us to the Guardian of the Threshold. Once the Guardian of the Threshold, at the edge of the abyss of being, has shown us how the forces of our inner humanity — willing, feeling, thinking — appear to the eyes of the Beings of the spiritual world; after the Guardian has shown us how in the present time's consciousness we have not awakened to our full humanity in respect to these forces if they are inwardly observed, but that these forces appear to the divine-spiritual powers as the three beasts, which are shown to us by the Guardian of the Threshold; after the Guardian of the Threshold has placed this shattering view before our souls, he shows us the path forward, which leads to ennoblement in self-knowledge, and which must be followed if the exhortation "O man, know thyself" is to be realized.

After he first showed us how we should stand in respect to our thinking, feeling and willing, he shows us — in the mantric verses which were cited at the end of the previous lesson in this Michael-School — how we are first to delve down into our thinking, but that this thinking is of a seeming nature [Scheineswesen] that cannot bear our true Self; but how we are then interwoven out in the cosmic ether and are at least able to revere those guiding beings [1] who lead us from earth-life to earth-life.

Then he shows us how we can delve down into feeling, how in feeling being and seeming are united, how there our being — selfhood in the good sense — arises with half its strength; how, however, we should understand that not only what is perishable and seeming in our being arises, but also the life-forces of the world, of the cosmos.

Only when we descend into the will do we feel being streaming into our selfhood. Seeming transforms itself into being. It descends into the will, and we feel the cosmic creating powers streaming through our will.

These were the Guardian of the Threshold's words at the edge of the abyss of being — where the yawning darkness, the night-cloaked darkness is still before us, which is to become light in order that we find the light that can illuminate our actual self. Behind us is the glowing, sunlit physical reality, which only becomes dark because we cannot find our actual being in it. There the Guardian of the Threshold says these mantric words:

See in yourself the weaving thoughts:
Seeming world is what you see,
Selfhood's being hides in you;
Delve down beneath the seeming:
Etheric essence flows in you;
Selfhood's being should revere the

Guiding Beings of your spirit.

Perceive within the flow of feeling:
Within you mingle seeming and being,
Your selfhood tends towards the seeming;
So plunge into your seeming being:
In you exist the cosmic-psychic forces;
Your selfhood then should understand
Your own soul's living powers.

Let strive with thrust of will
Which rises out of all the seeming,
With creative actual Self it rises;
Your life in full should turn to it:
It is filled with cosmic-spirit-force;
Your inner Self should truly grasp
Creative cosmic force in the spirit-I.

[The mantra is written on the blackboard.]

The Guardian speaks:

See in yourself the weaving thoughts:
Seeming world is what you see,
Selfhood's being hides in you;
Delve down beneath the seeming:
Etheric essence flows in you;
Selfhood's being should revere the
Guiding Beings of your spirit.

Perceive within the flow of feeling:
Within you mingle seeming and being,
Your selfhood tends towards the seeming;
So plunge into your seeming being:
In you exist the cosmic-psychic forces;
Your selfhood then should understand
Your own soul's living powers.

Let strive within the thrust of will
Rising out of all the seeming
With creative actual self it rises;
Your life in full should turn to it:
It's filled with cosmic-spirit-force;
Your inner self should truly grasp
Creative cosmic force in the spirit-I.

The Guardian of the Threshold has spoken a mantric verse to us, of which we should not only receive its content, but rather with our whole feeling we should enter into the weave and life of the spiritual world. Therefore, this mantric verse is shaped so that in its rhythm it appears as having moved downward from the spiritual world. Each line begins with a stressed syllable, followed by an unstressed syllable. So, we have in the first verse:

[While speaking the trochaic rhythm symbols (—∪) are placed above the first syllables of each line and then spoken with the appropriate stress]

See in yourself the weaving thoughts:
Seeming world is what you see,
Selfhood's being hides in you;
Delve down beneath the seeming:
Etheric essence flows in you;
Selfhood's being should revere the
Guiding Beings of your spirit.

This coming down by the spiritual world to us is to be felt in the trochaic rhythm. Only then do we receive this verse correctly in our souls. Only when this speaking down to us by the spiritual world is with this intonation do we receive this verse in our souls correctly, feeling it deeply within us:

See in yourself the weaving thoughts:
Seeming world is what you see,
Selfhood's being hides in you;
Delve down beneath the seeming:
Etheric essence flows in you;
Selfhood's being should revere the
Guiding Beings of your spirit.

The next verse is the opposite: Now we should rise with our feeling to being. Here [the first syllable] we are below: here [the second syllable] we strive upward to being: The unstressed [low] tone is before the stressed [high] tone:

[while speaking, the iambic rhythm symbols (∪—) are placed over the first two syllables of each line, and it is spoken with the corresponding intonation:]

Perceive within the flow of feeling:
Within you mingle seeming and being,
Your selfhood tends towards the seeming;
So plunge into your seeming being:
In you exist the cosmic-psychic forces;
Your selfhood then should understand
Your own soul's living powers.

We must live in these words, which are mantrically united in this rhythm:

Perceive within the flow of feeling:
Within you mingle seeming and being,
Your selfhood tends towards the seeming;
So plunge into your seeming being:
In you exist the cosmic-psychic forces;
Your selfhood then should understand
Your own soul's living powers.

That we have entered in reality is expressed in that we first "revere", which is an inner soul function; in that we then "understand", where we gradually come alongside the process; in that we first arrive at the "guiding Beings", who are to guide us; then the "living powers", which weave and live through life. In one mantric verse all is in the right place and all is integrated in the organism of the whole.

The third verse tells us how we perceive being directly in the will. We stand alongside being. Two high-toned syllables begin:

[While speaking the spondaic symbols (— —) are placed over the first two syllables of each line on the blackboard and the lines are spoken with the corresponding emphasis:

Let strive within the thrust of will
Rising out of all the sham
With creative actual self it rises;
Your life in full should turn to it:
It's filled with cosmic-spirit-force;
Your inner self should truly grasp
Creative cosmic force in the spirit-I.

We have now come farther. It is no longer "understand"; It is "grasp", which is an action. The "Creative cosmic force" instead of "living powers" is placed at the beginning of the line to indicate the complete reversal we make when rising from "sham" to "being".

The beginning of each line of the third verse is therefore to be felt in its spondaic rhythm. Here we have trochaic ["trochaic" is written alongside the first verse]; here iambic ["iambic" is written alongside the second verse]; here spondaic ["spondaic" is written alongside the third verse].

Let strive within the thrust of will
Which rises out of all the seeming
With creative actual self it rises;
Your life in full should turn to it:
It's filled with cosmic-spirit-force;
Your inner self should truly grasp
Creative cosmic force in the spirit-I.

After the Guardian of the Threshold has presented this to our souls, he makes us aware of how we should integrate ourselves into the cosmos, into the world with all its forces if we want to advance in spiritual knowledge. For what is within us is at first not distinguishable according to its place, whereas in the cosmos it is ordered. In the cosmos, we can indicate the definite place. Within us everything is interwoven. But we do not achieve real knowledge if we do not rise up to the cosmic forces and the cosmic powers — if we remain subjective in ourselves, remaining in our own skin, if we do not go out of ourselves and let our body become the whole world. Then will our soul, our narrow humanity, feel itself to be a member of the cosmos. The spirit will integrate our narrow humanity into the whole cosmos, into the whole world.

We must carry this out, as the Guardian of the Threshold indicates when he shows us how from the depths of the earth, which draws all the beings by gravity, forces arise which also draw us down, which bind our will to the earth if we don't make ourselves free by inner striving. Our gaze goes earthward if we want to localize our will. We must feel ourselves one with the earth's gravity, feel drawn by the earth and make the effort to free ourselves from the earth's gravity if we want to let our will to be one with the cosmos.

> Feel how the depths of earth
> Thrust their forces on your being,
> On the members of your body.
> You will lose yourself in them
> If your willing trusts itself
> Powerlessly to their striving;
> They would darken in you the I.

Thus, speaks the Guardian of the Threshold to our willing on behalf of Michael at the yawning abyss of being.

And in wanting to integrate our feeling into the cosmos, he does not direct us to the depths, but to the horizontal reaches of the world, where the forces swing from west to east, from east to west, permeating us. These are the same forces that grasp our feeling. We must feel the divine godly powers, who send their spiritual light in these pulsing waves from the horizontal directions if we wish to integrate our feeling into the cosmic distance. In order to integrate our willing into the vertical, feel it bound below and freed above, we must be able to send our feeling into the cosmic distance. Then there will be light in our feeling. Then something goes through our feeling which also goes through us, just as the sun illuminates the earth's air when it moves from east to west.

However, in all that streams through us we must be loving. The force of love alone, which lives and courses through humanity, can accomplish what is asked of us. Then wisdom will course through us, and we will feel ourselves to be in the wide circles in which the sun moves, as feeling humanity, as Self, strong for true, good spiritual creativity.

In respect to feeling, the Guardian of the Threshold, at the yawning abyss of being, says this to us as feeling human beings:

> Feel how from the cosmic distance
> Godly powers their spiritual light
> Let illuminate your psychic being.
> Be yourself loving in them, and
> They'll create, wisdom-weaving,
> You as Self within their circles,
> Strong for the good, spirit creating.

And when the Guardian of the Threshold wants to speak to our thinking so that it integrates itself in the cosmos, he doesn't direct us down to the will, which should rise upward; he doesn't direct us to feeling in the wide circle in which the sun moves, but he indicates the heights, the heavenly heights where alone the self can live selflessly if it wants to receive the powers of thought in what comes with grace from above, if it wants to follow a higher striving. We stand below, the Word is above. We must be inwardly courageous to hear the Word, for only if we courageously strive for wisdom and knowledge does the cosmic Word resound from above, full of grace, speaking about humanity's true wisdom.

Again, the Guardian of the Threshold speaks to us at the yawning abyss of being:

> Feel how in heavenly heights
> Selfhood can selflessly live,
> When it wants, striving to follow,
> Spirit-filled, powers of thought,
> And courageously hear the Word
> That resounds with grace from above
> Into the true being of man.

[The mantra is written on the blackboard.]

The Guardian instructs us on Willing, Feeling, Thinking:

> *Feel how the depths of earth*
> *Thrust their forces on your being,*
> *On the members of your body.*
> *You will lose yourself in them*
> *If your willing trusts itself*
> *Powerlessly to their striving;*
> *They would darken in you the I.*
>
> *Feel how from the cosmic distance*
> *Godly powers their spiritual light*
> *Let illuminate your psychic being.*

Be yourself loving in them,
And they'll create, wisdom-weaving,
You as Self within their circles,
Strong for the good, spirit creating.

Feel how in heavenly heights
Selfhood can selflessly live,
When it wants, striving, to follow,
Spirit filled, powers of thought,
And courageously hear the Word
That resounds with grace from above
Into the true being of man.

We must look above if our thinking wants to unite itself with the forces of the cosmos. The realm of cosmic circling distance is where we must feel ourselves to be if our feeling wants to unite itself with the cosmic forces. Below is the place where we must look to insert our earthbound willing, which we should make free above, into the cosmic realms. Everywhere — above, in the distance and below — everywhere is special Being. We must feel it. The Guardian of the Threshold, on behalf of Michael, points us there and he tells us what we'll find above, in the middle and below.

He instructs us further about the heights, the middle and below, because he wants to instruct us about thinking, feeling and willing. This is what he says:

The light does battle with gloomy powers
In that realm, where your thinking
In spirit-being longs to enter.
You find, striving lightward,
Your Self, taken from you by spirit;
You can, if darkness entices you,
The Self in matter lose.

We are placed between light and darkness. Light wants our Self, darkness wants our Self. We are to find the path between light and darkness to come to the Self. That is what lies in the Guardian of the Threshold's admonition.

Th Guardian speaks to our feeling:

The warmth does battle with the cold
In that realm, where your feeling would
In spirit-interweaving live.
You find, loving warmth, your Self
In spirit-longing blown away;
You can, if cold does harden you,
The Self in sorrow grind to dust.

Again, we are standing between polar opposites with our feeling: between the loving warmth, between warm love and cold hardness, the hardening cold. We must find the path between them if our Self would find itself.

And about the third realm, where the will originates, the Guardian of the Threshold admonishes us:

> Thus, life does battle with death
> In that realm, where your will
> Would act with spiritual creation.
> You find, holding on to life,
> Your Self vanishing in spirit's power;
> If death's power binds you fast,
> You can your Self constrict to nothing.

Life and death: We can lose our will to life, we can lose it to death; in life feel it vanish, in death feel it constricted.

We must seek for the path. The Guardian urges us to do so. It will be the subject we begin with in the next lesson.

The Guardian once more points out how we must seek the path to arrive at our human Self. He speaks with earnest words, for it is not easy to find the inner strength that holds and carries and leads the Self to find what it does not have in normal earthly life. We will see later how the Guardian gives us the means to do so.

Next Saturday, when this mantric verse will be written on the blackboard, we will hear the Guardian further as he gradually points out the ways we can go astray — which we must know about in order to find the right path.

*

But now we must again consider, looking back at earthly life — which we must do every time we enter the esoteric — so now let us again consider the admonition which was spoken to humankind in the past by all the Beings and events, which speaks to humankind in the present and which will speak to humankind in the future:

> O man, know thyself!
> So resounds the Cosmic-Word.
> You hear it strong in soul,
> You feel it firm in spirit.
>
> Who speaks with such cosmic might?
> Who speaks with such depth of heart?
>
> Does it work through distant radiant space

Into your senses' sense of being?
Does it ring through weaving waves of time
Into your life's evolving stream?

It's you yourself who,
In feeling space, in experiencing time,

Create the Word, feeling foreign
In the soulless void of space
Because you lose the force of thought
In time's destructive flow.

When all that streams through this Michael-School from the Guardian on Michael's behalf, when here the instruction in the rightfully existent Michael-School penetrates our soul, then we may be sure, if we are honest and open minded, that Michael's strength will stream through this room, which may be indicated by Michael's sign:

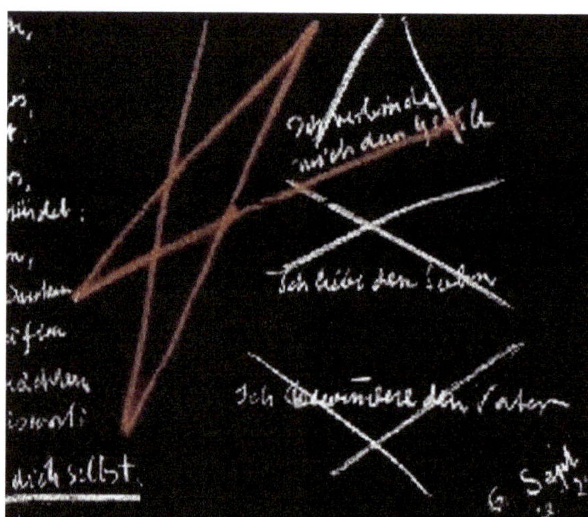

[in red]

and by the seal-gestures, through which Michael lets the RoseCross stream enter the RoseCross temple, the strength which humanity needs today for its esoteric life, which here acts from the threefold source of the cosmos — from the divine Father-principle, from the Christ-principle, from the principle of the Spirit, so that the RoseCross verse is united with the Michael-Gesture-seal:

Ex deo nascimur

[lower seal-gesture]

In Christo morimur

[middle seal-gesture]

Per spiritum sanctum reviviscimus

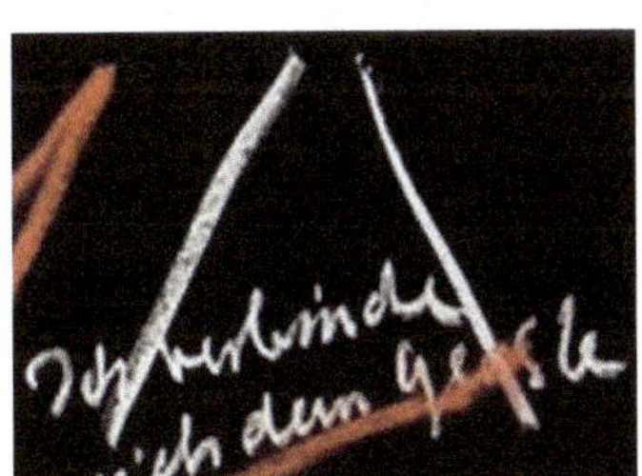

[upper seal-gesture]

which must be felt so that the gestures are understood as:

I revere the Father

[lower seal-gesture]

I love the son

[middle seal-gesture]

I unite with the spirit

[upper seal-gesture]

Once more:

[Michael-Sign-Gesture]

[together with the seal-gestures is spoken:]

Ex deo nascimur

In Christo morimur

Per spiritum sanctum reviviscimus

*

The mantric verses which are given in this School may only be possessed by those who are members of this School. In the case of someone who is a member of the School and is not present during a lesson, so does not have the verses, he can obtain them from another member who has them. For this it is necessary to request permission from Dr. [Ita] Wegman or from me. So, when someone wants to receive the verses because he was not able to have them here, it is necessary to ask either Dr. Wegman or me. But not the one who wants them is to ask, but the one who gives them. This must be said as a foregone conclusion.

This is not some administrative measure, but in every case where the verses are passed on this must be observed, because it is the start of the occult act through which the verses are received.

Those members who have recently joined may only receive the verses up to the lesson in which they have participated. Only in special cases, which must be judged individually, may the request be made for the later verses to be given. By mail — that is, by a means other than verbally — the verses may not be passed on from one to another.

If anyone should write down anything else but the verses, he is obliged to only keep what he has written for a week, and then burn it. What is communicated here in the rightfully existing Michael School only has importance through verbal communication — this is an inner occult law —, with the exception of the mantric verses.

It must be understood, so that these things are not thought to be childishly oriented towards sectarianism, that if these occult verses are passed on to others in a way that is not permissible, they lose their effectiveness, for the act of passing on belongs to the effectiveness of the School. It is because of these occult facts that the handling of the verses is so strictly required.

*

The activities for tomorrow are: At 10:30 a.m. the course for Pastoral Medicine; in the afternoon at 3:30 p.m. the course for theologians; in the evening a lecture for members, and at 5 p.m. a eurythmy performance. The speech course is at 12 o'clock as usual.

[1] According to the stenographic notes, “guiding being” is singular here. However, later, and in other places, the plural is used, “guiding Beings”. The meaning here seems also to be plural. [trans.]

Lesson Four
(recapitulation)

Dornach, September 13, 1924

My dear sisters and brothers,

It is not possible every time to give the corresponding introduction about the task and meaning of the School and about membership in the School. Therefore, although a large number of new members are again present, I will not give the introduction, but will continue from where we left off last time, and I must remind the members who are to give the previous mantras to the newcomers in the usual way, that they must to do so under the conditions which I will mention at the end of this lesson. They should also describe the conditions for acceptance in this School.

*

We shall begin by again letting our souls hear the words which are spoken by all the Beings and processes of the world to the human being who wishes to be worthy of the name, and who has an unbiased sense that in them lies the exhortation to seek true self-knowledge, a self-knowledge that leads to knowledge of the world. And we are exhorted from all sides, from all the Beings of all the kingdoms of nature and all the kingdoms of spirit to this self-knowledge in the true sense of the word, which is the path to world-knowledge. Thus, all the Beings of nature and of the spirit exhorted humans in the past, exhort them in the present, and will exhort humans in the future. These exhorting words that urge the soul of man, if he wants to hear them, from all sides, from the east and the west, from the south and the north, from above and below, may also today begin to describe what this Michael-School should mean:

O man, know thyself!
So resounds the Cosmic-Word.
You hear it strong in soul,
You feel it firm in spirit.

Who speaks with such cosmic might?
Who speaks with such depth of heart?

Does it work through distant radiant space
Into your senses' sense of being?
Does it ring through weaving waves of time
Into your life's evolving stream?

It's you yourself who,
In feeling space, in experiencing time,

Create the Word, feeling foreign
In the soulless void of space

Because you lose the force of thought
In time's destructive flow.

*

We have seen how the seeker of knowledge approaches the Guardian of the Threshold, how — after the seeker of knowledge has stood there shattered by the impression of the three beasts, which show the true nature of his present willing, feeling and thinking as they appear before the visage of the spiritual world — how he is gradually lifted up by the Guardian of the Threshold.

And we have already heard what the Guardian of the Threshold speaks to the one he wants to lift up, how he points, on the one hand, above, where a battle is taking place between the light and the dark powers in the realm from which the force of our thinking streams into our humanity. The Guardian of the Threshold thinks that we need this image. We need — if we wish to feel in the right way, by seeking knowledge, the origins of our thinking, the force of our thinking in our humanity — to look up to that realm from which our thinking comes, where however a terrible battle rages between the powers of light, the light which wants to guide thinking along the right track, and the powers of darkness, who want to divert thinking from the right track and lead it along paths of aberration. Our thinking is rooted above. We must know it to be so rooted if we want to be knowledgeable in the battle between light and darkness.

And then, if we understand what striving towards the light is, we find that we must remain erect. And we must know that we are involved with the battle between light and darkness: The light wants to bring us to a state of spiritual powerlessness, so to speak; the darkness wants to make us lose ourselves in matter. But we must seek the state of equilibrium between them — not letting ourselves be overtaken by light, nor letting the darkness transform us into matter, but to stand firmly in our selfhood and find the equilibrium for our thinking between light and darkness.

And then when we consider our feeling, we must see — in that realm which reaches out into the horizontal, into the cosmic distances — how we are involved in the battle between the warmth of soul and the coldness of soul.

In the warmth of soul are working all the luciferic powers, the powers of beauty, the powers of brightness, the powers who want to give us divine forces without our own effort. We would be unfree and lacking independence if they were to catch us.

But on the other side are the powers of cold, the coldness of soul that is permeated by ahrimanic Beings who would cause us to lose our Selves in the cold. We must find the equilibrium between that spiritual blissfulness into which the forces of warmth, the forces of heat, of fire wish to bring us, and that region into which, with enormous all-embracing intellectuality, the ahrimanic powers wish to seduce us with coldness. We must maintain our equilibrium between both of them in order to find the right sense of feeling for knowledge.

Then, when we observe our willing, we must look below. There is the realm of the earth and of gravity from which the force of our will comes for our earthly life. For the earth does not only contain the force of gravity; spiritually, it also contains the force of human will. Once again, we stand face to face with two powers — the powers of life and the powers of death. We can succumb with our willing to the powers of life. Then it is as though the powers of life want to seize us, use our will forces in the cosmos. We must hold our Self erect, and find the equilibrium between these powers of life and the powers of death, the latter wanting to confine us in a constricted space in order to eternally interweave our will with materiality.

The Guardian of the Threshold exhorts us at this point to maintain ourselves in equilibrium between light and darkness, in equilibrium between warmth and cold, in equilibrium between life and death. For we may not only belong to the power of the light. In light alone we would be benumbed, dazzled. We may not devote ourselves to the darkness alone, for then we would lose ourselves in the substance of darkness. We must strive for what is striven for in all the world.

Wherever you look, my sisters and brothers, light and darkness intermingle. Look at your hair. The light plants it in your head. But it must be permeated with darkness, otherwise your hair would be entirely rays of light. Look at your whole body: it is woven of light. But it could have no solidity if darkness were not also interwoven in it. Look at any object, my sisters and brothers! Blossoming plants: they are created from light; but the powers of darkness must press up from the soil so that from light and darkness what the plants represent in their solid consistency — the nature of plants on earth — can be found.

Just as in all of nature a balance between light and darkness is found, so must the human being strive psychically for it in the spiritual world if he wants to be a real seeker after knowledge. And it is also the case for equilibrium between warmth and cold, and for equilibrium between life and death.

So, there we are at the yawning abyss of being, still looking, as behind us the gleaming colorful kingdoms of nature, to which we belong with our senses, become darker and darker as it becomes clear to us that our real being is not revealed by all of wondrous sensory nature, nor is it what leads us to self-knowledge. In front of us, like a black wall, is still the border of the dark realm, into which we must go so that there will be light within by means of the force which we ourselves bring. We are still standing at the yawning abyss of being, but have become bolder in confidence that through the Guardian's admonitions we will grow wings to cross the abyss in order to enter the darkness, and there is light in the darkness.

This is one of the last of the Guardian's admonitions:

> The light does battle with powers of darkness
> In that realm, where your thinking
> In spirit-being longs to enter.
> You find, striving lightward,
> Your Self, taken from you by spirit;
> You can, when darkness entices you,
> The Self in matter lose.
>
> The warmth does battle with the cold

In that realm, where your feeling would
In spirit-interweaving live.
You find, loving warmth, your Self
In spirit-longing blown away;
You can, if cold does harden you,
The Self in sorrow grind to dust.

Thus, life does battle with death
In that realm where your will
Would act with spiritual creation.
You find, holding on to life,
Your Self vanishing in spirit's power;
If death's power binds you fast,
You may constrict the Self to nothing.

[The mantra is written on the blackboard.]

The Guardian at the abyss exacting equilibrium:

The light does battle with powers of darkness
In that realm where your thinking
In spirit-being longs to enter.
You find, striving lightward,
Your Self, taken from you by spirit;
You can, when darkness entices you,
The Self in matter lose.

The warmth does battle with the cold
In that realm, where your feeling would
In spirit-interweaving live.
You find, loving warmth, your Self
In spirit-longing blown away;
You can, if cold does harden you,
The Self in sorrow grind to dust.

Thus, life does battle with death
In that realm, where your will
Would act with spiritual creation.
You find, holding on to life,
Your Self vanishing in spirit's power;
If death's power binds you fast,
You may constrict the Self to nothing.

You will find, my dear sisters and brothers, that if you devote yourselves to these mantric worlds with the right conviction and with peace in your souls, with a feeling of sacrificial devotion to the spirit, you will find that what instills equilibrium in the soul is present in the words themselves.

As seekers after knowledge, we stand now before the Guardian of the Threshold at the yawning abyss of being. Next the Guardian of the Threshold teaches us how we, in wanting to choose the right direction between light and darkness, warmth and cold, life and death, can find our own Self.

In no other way can we do this, my dear sisters and brothers, than by pondering the following: In order to achieve true knowledge it is necessary that we become one with the world, that we have a feeling respecting the world as a finger would if it could feel for itself, feel itself to be a part of the entire human body. If the finger could feel for itself it would say: I am only a finger as long as I am a part of the human body, when the human body's blood is my blood, when the human body's pulsation is my pulsation. If I am cut off, I cease being a finger. The finger loses its meaning when separated from the organism to which it belongs and only as part of which it can be a finger.

The human being must learn to feel in this way in respect to the entire world. We are members of the spirit-soul organism of the entire world, and only seem to be separated from the spirit-soul organism of the world. We must connect in the right way to the spirit-soul organism of the world and must know that around us the elements earth, water, air, fire are spread, and we must learn to feel that our bodily nature — for it is composed of these elements — is at one with these elements.

The Guardian of the Threshold teaches us that we should do this, and how. Just consider exactly what learning streams in those mantric verses the Guardian of the Threshold has given us, which have brought us to the abyss of being.

My dear sisters and brothers, think that you tentatively touch some object with your finger. You know that the object is there where you touch it. You touch an object. You have the feeling of being at one with this object, because at the moment you touch it the sense of touch is what makes a finger, or whatever you touch it with, at one with the object. Now think that you as a whole are like a finger, a touching finger. You are standing on the earth, on the element earth. You are standing here because the earth's main property is the element of gravity. You are touching the earth with the soles of your feet, regardless of whether you are standing on the floor of a room or outside on the bare earth. The point is that you feel, in standing, that you are touching the earth's gravitational element. You could be standing above on a mountain, or on a tower: you sense — just as you sense at the tip of your finger the hard and the soft, the warm and the cold — in the process of touching you sense the unity in your soles of your feet, where you sense the weight of gravity.

The Guardian of the Threshold says this when he admonishes us in the following way:

> O man, touch within your body's entire being
> How earthly forces support you in existence.

That earthly forces are our support, that the earthly element supports us so we don't sink down, is what the Guardian of the Threshold is telling us now.

Then he leads us further, so that we not only feel that we are like a whole finger, but that we also feel what is within the finger: it is the element of water, of fluid. For everything which is in the human being — something also known by physical science — is born from the fluid element. Solid is isolated from fluid, as ice is from water. We must rise to the sensation of the element of water. Out in the world everything is of a fluid nature. Our own formative forces are formed in us by the fluid element. Just as we feel the earth as our support, we also feel, in that we feel our organs, that we are formed as human beings out of the fluid element. It creates the formative forces for us. Our lungs and our livers are solidly formed, but they solidify from out of the fluid element, from out of the element of water. Just as we feel the earth to be our support, we also feel, in that we feel our organs, that the water element forms us as human beings. The water forces are our sculptors; the earth is our support. Therefore, the Guardian of the Threshold admonishes us:

O man, experience in the circle of your touch

(We can touch everywhere, but when we feel the touching itself ...)

O man, experience in the circle of your touch,
How water-beings are your being's sculptors.

Now the Guardian of the Threshold continues to admonish us. He teaches us how we can also unite with the powers of air. We breathe in the air. We know that if we breathe in the air in the wrong way we feel it; so, it has to do with our feelings. We have feelings that make us fearful, that breech the coherence of our existence. Just as the water element shapes us, so do does the air element care for us. The Guardian of the Threshold admonishes us:

O man, now feel in all your life's interweaving
How powers of air are your caregivers in existence.

Now the Guardian leads us farther on to the warmth element. We feel ourselves united internally with warmth. We feel the earth outside of us as support. We know little about how the water forces shape us, during growth, for example; that stays in the subconscious. The powers of air thrust themselves in only when they are abnormal, when they don't work normally. But we feel united with warmth when we have the right amount in us. Our souls and our whole being become warm when we feel warmth from without. We stiffen when we must experience cold from without. Warmth and cold are at one with us in a completely different way in the elemental world. There they are neither merely supporters, nor our sculptors, nor our caregivers — they are our true helpers in physical existence. The Guardian of the Threshold admonishes us:

O man, think in all the streams of feeling,
How fire-powers are helpers in your existence.

If we heed all that is entailed in these demands, we will find the path to conscious unification of our corporeality with the elements. And in different degrees our corporeality is one with the elements. At first the earth-element supports us in an exterior, mechanical way. The earth-element is support for us; it is mechanical and exterior. It will become more inward, but still consists of formations which do not reach the soul; water-beings form us, are our “sculptors”. When we become one with the air-elements, we rise to the level of morality. The air-element is no longer a mere exterior designer, it is our caregiver. And our feelings are of anxiety if we do not breathe in the right way. The powers of air are “caregivers”; warmth and cold are “helpers”, enabling us to be earthly beings. They are fire-powers, now wholly at the moral level.

The summation of the Guardian of the Threshold's admonitions with respect to the escalation of the elements:

O man, observe yourself in the elemental kingdom.

[The mantra is written on the blackboard.]

The Guardian's teaching:

O man, touch within your body's entire being
How earthly forces support you in existence.

O man, experience in all the circle of your touch,>
How water-beings are your being's sculptors.

O man, now feel in all your life's interweaving
How powers of air are your caregivers in existence.

O man, think in all the streams of feeling,
How fire-powers are helpers in your existence.

We have here the escalation [the words are underlined on the blackboard.]: “support”, “sculptors”, “caregivers”, “helpers”.

We also have another escalation. For in a mantric verse every word is in the right place, and there is no word there that only serves to fill an empty space. Everything coincides with its inner meaning with which we should unite ourselves in meditation on the mantric verse. We have an escalation [underlined on the blackboard] “touch”, “experience”, “feel”, “think”. It is a special escalation. So in meditation we must also sense the inner, meaningful structure of such a mantric verse.

Once the Guardian has said this, he sums it up again in one line:

[It is written on the blackboard:]

O man, observe yourself in the elemental kingdom.

Thus, the Guardian leads us to an inner experience of the verses, through which we can unite our corporeality with the elements to which it belongs.

Then he guides us further on to the soul. Here he doesn't point us to the elements earth, water, air, fire; here he points us to the planets. He points out to us how we should feel about what mutually draws the planets' orbits around the earth, how one planet or another draws the orbit. The orbits have a relationship and speak to each other when the human being rises in his soul to this secret of the universe-pointing, planetary powers. Then he lives with his soul in the spiritual kingdom of the cosmos, just as he had previously lived with his body in the elemental kingdom. We can only psychically feel to be at one with the cosmos if we bring ourselves to live into the kingdom of the planets and their orbits. The Guardian of the Threshold tells us this with these words:

O man, let rule within your depths of soul
The universe-pointing planetary powers.

[It is written on the blackboard.]

O man, let rule within your depths of soul
The universe-pointing planetary powers.

Again, the Guardian of the Threshold sums up the direction-giving forces in these two lines for how the soul can feel to be at one with the secrets of the planets:

[written on the blackboard]

> *O man, become yourself...*
> (which means: make yourself existent)
> *... through the cosmic orbits.*

The cosmic orbits of the various planets are drawn together into one cosmic orbit. We have thereby felt body and soul to be at one with the cosmos: the body with the earthly elements, the soul with the planets.

If we want the spirit to feel at one with the universe, we can neither look to the elements nor to the secrets of the planets, rather must we look to the stars. For there is the power with which we must feel our spirit to be at one with in the distant universe, if we wish to feel ourselves to be members of this universe in the true sense. There the cosmos begins to intone the music of the spheres. Therefore, the Guardian of the Threshold admonishes us:

> O man, preserve within your spirit's creation
> The planets' words proclaimed in heaven.

[It is written on the blackboard.]

> *O man, preserve within your spirit's creation*
> *The planets' words proclaimed in heaven.*

Again, the Guardian of the Threshold summarizes the requirement in one line:

> O man, create yourself through heaven's wisdom.

> Every moment our spiritual existence is a creation of our Self.

[It is written on the blackboard.]

> *At every moment our spiritual existence is a creation of our Self.*

If we sense and feel this in the right way, we are internalized by the Guardian of the Threshold. We recall how the words of self-knowledge were intoned from all creation still in an abstract form, how they rang out to us from all sides of natural and spiritual existence. But now the phrase: “O man, know thyself”, is clarified in all its parts. It now consists of one, two, three, four, five, six, seven, eight, nine parts.

“O man, know thyself” should be seen as nine rays of light, so to speak. Then it will be filled with what our meditation needs.

That is how we should feel. And, in a certain sense, we should pledge to the Guardian of the Threshold that we will adhere to his admonition:

O man, touch within your body's entire being
How earthly forces support you in existence.

O man, experience in all the circle of your touch,
How water-beings are your being's sculptors.

O man, now feel in all your life's interweaving
How powers of air are your caregivers in existence.

O man, think in all the streams of feeling,
How fire-powers are helpers in your existence.

O man, observe yourself in the elemental kingdom.

O man, let rule within your depths of soul
The universe-pointing planetary powers.

O man, become yourself through the cosmic orbits.

O man, preserve within your spirit's creation
The planets' words proclaimed in heaven.

O man, create yourself through heaven's wisdom.

We make a kind of pledge to the Guardian of the Threshold that we will always adhere to his admonitions, letting them run through our soul as mantras.

Again, and again we look back, and at every step we feel bound to remember what is happening on this side of the threshold. And on this side of the threshold every stone and every plant, every tree, every cloud, every spring, every rock, every lightning, every thunder has called to us:

O man, know thyself!
So resounds the Cosmic-Word.
You hear it strong in soul,
You feel it firm in spirit.

Who speaks with such cosmic might?
Who speaks with such depth of heart?

Does it work through distant radiant space
Into your senses' sense of being?
Does it ring through weaving waves of time
Into your life's evolving stream?

It's you yourself who,
In feeling space, in experiencing time,

Create the Word, feeling foreign
In the soulless void of space
Because you lose the force of thought
In time's destructive flow.

Thus, when these words of the Guardian of the threshold ring out with full spiritual force in this room — words which he as the serving member of Michael's power, the reigning power of our time — when these words ring out we can be certain, because this esoteric school has been founded by Michael's might itself, that Michael is present with his force, with his spirit, with his love, that Michael is psycho-spiritually present among us.

And that can be confirmed — here where responsibility is felt by the leadership of the School towards the power of Michael — that nothing else streams through this School than what is present in the holy will of Michael. It may be confirmed by Michael's sign and Michael's seal; this Michael-Sign [in red]:

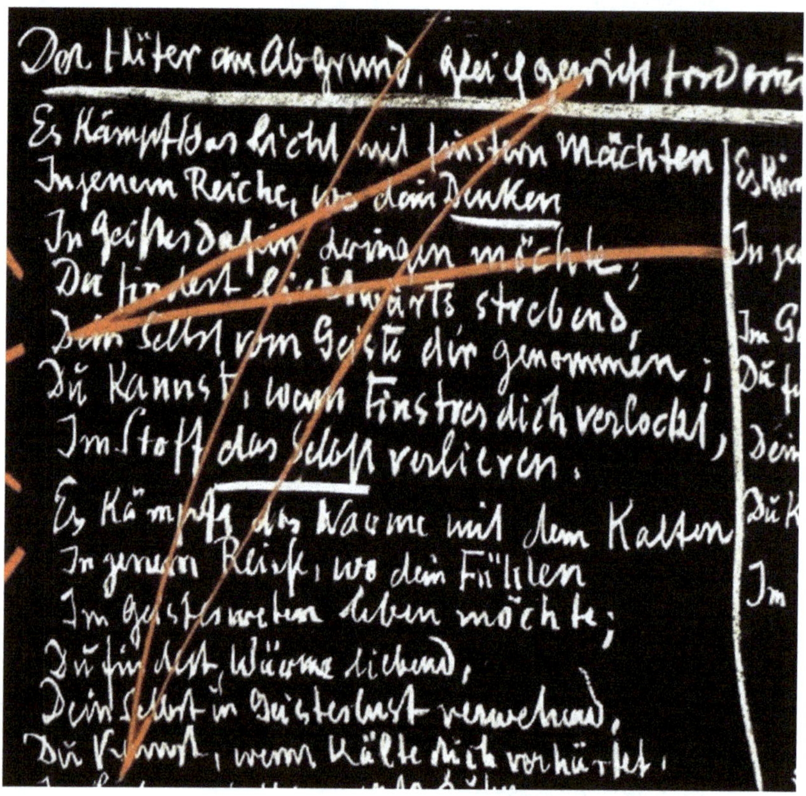

and the Michael-seal, which confirms that Michael-Power enters into the true Rosicrucian training and is thus conjoined with what is being taught in the Michael School with Michael's seal, which the Rosicrucian endowment seals in the Rosicrucian verse accompanied by the seal-signs:

Ex deo nascimur

[seal gesture]

In Cristo morimur

[seal gesture]

Per spiritum sanctum reviviscimus

[seal gesture]

and that means:

I revere the Father

[first seal gesture]

I love the Son

[middle seal gesture]

I unite with the Spirit

[third seal gesture]

“I revere the Father”: in saying “Ex deo nascimur”, this feeling passes through our soul;

“I love the Son”: in saying “In Cristo morimur”, this feeling passes silently through our soul;

“I unite with the Spirit”: is silently felt when saying “Per spiritum sanctum reviviscimus”.

The mantric verses come to you, my sisters and brothers, with the sign and seal of Michael:

[Michael Sign]

[Together with the seal gestures is spoken:]

Ex deo nascimur

In Cristo morimur

Per spiritum sanctum reviviscimus.

*

Only those who have been accepted as members of this School may possess the verses which are imparted here. Those who cannot be present during a lesson when verses have been given, may receive them from those who have received them in the School itself. However, in order to receive the verses, permission must first be granted by either Dr. Wegman or by me. The request to Dr. Wegman or to me can only be made by the one who wants to give the verses to another. Therefore, the one who wants to receive them should not request them; it would serve no purpose. He can go to someone and ask that he be given them; but the one who gives them must ask permission in every case. This is not an administrative rule, but an occult arrangement which must be followed, because the handing over must begin with this real act.

The request may not be done in writing — it has happened, so I must be clear about it — but must be done orally, except when exceptional circumstances make an oral understanding impossible. Least of all in esoteric matters should even the hint of bureaucracy exist. Everything must be alive, just as it should be in the Anthroposophical Society.

Furthermore, whoever writes down more than the verses is obliged to keep what has been written for only one week and then to burn it. For it is not good that they somehow remain longer. They can go in all possible directions. Esoteric material must be handled in this way; it is not an arbitrary rule. In esoterica, everything is determined from true occult foundations. And if esoteric mantric verses are revealed in an incorrect way by the members who have the right because they either received the verses here during a lesson or by the correct way as described — if they are received by others in an incorrect way, they lose all their spiritual force. That is an occult law. And in the spiritual world there are laws which may not be ignored without punishment. So, this is not an arbitrary rule, but one which obeys an occult law.

*

Now for some announcements. Tomorrow at 9:30 a.m. the course about Pastoral Medicine will continue, then at 12 noon the course for Speech Formation and drama; in the afternoon at 3:30 p.m. the course for Theologians. At 5 p.m. there will be an eurythmy performance. The next Esoteric Lesson, in which the Michael teachings will be rounded out, will take place on Monday at 8:30.

Lesson Five
(recapitulation)

Dornach, September 15, 1924

My Dear Sisters and Brothers,

New members have again come to this School today. It isn't possible to repeat every time the introduction which describes the duties and meaning of this Michael School. Therefore, I ask the members who wish to give the verses to the new members, to do so in the manner I will describe at the end of the Lesson, and to give them the introduction, which everyone who wishes to be a member of this School must necessarily know.

*

And so, we will also begin directly today to inscribe in our souls the words which sound forth, to those who are open-minded enough, from all the kingdoms of nature and the hierarchies of the world which surround us as human beings. In the past, these words sounded forth to man from all the stones and plants, clouds, stars, from the sun and the moon, from the springs and the rocks. They sound forth to him in the present; they will sound forth to him in the future.

O man, know thyself!
So resounds the Cosmic-Word.
You hear it strong in soul,
You feel it firm in spirit.

Who speaks with such cosmic might?
Who speaks with such depth of heart?

Does it work through distant radiant space
Into your senses' sense of being?
Does it ring through weaving waves of time
Into your life's evolving stream?

It's you yourself who,
In feeling space, in experiencing time,

Create the Word, feeling foreign
In space's soulless void
Because you lose the force of thought
In time's destroying flow.

My dear sisters and brothers, in the description of the path of knowledge we have reached the place where we stand before the Guardian at the abyss of being. The Guardian of the Threshold has made clear to us that what surrounds us in the exterior world can never reveal our own being to us; how our observation of nature, what on and from the earth lives and moves, what shines and speaks from the realm of the stars — to the extent we can perceive it with the senses and with our reason — all that offers nothing to clarify the being of our own self; that the brightness, this glistening in the sunshine, this living and interweaving which is so grand and powerful, so beautiful and magnificent in the outer world, remains dark and gloomy for our true self-knowledge.

Then it was described how we approach the Guardian little by little, who appears to us in the figure of a spiritual cloud, thus showing us an image of ourselves, which in turn shows us what we should strive for as human beings in order to achieve self-knowledge.

Then we reached the Guardian of the Threshold. He showed us what the true shape of our willing, feeling and thinking is before the countenance of the gods. He showed us how being fainthearted and having fear of knowledge lives in us, as hate for knowledge, as doubt about the knowledge that is nevertheless in us, because the character of our times has driven it into us. He showed us the animal form of our willing, feeling and thinking. It must be a shattering experience for us when the Guardian of the Threshold awakens the forces which lead to true self-knowledge in our souls.

Then the Guardian of the Threshold raised us, first showing us, however, how our thinking, as we use it in normal life, is the corpse of the living thinking which was in us before we descended to physical-sensory existence. He showed us how our body, in earthly existence, is a coffin for the deceased living thinking, which lies in the coffin as a corpse. But we use this corpse for our usual abstract thinking between birth and death in order to understand the things of the physical-sensory world.

Once we grasp how dead this thinking is, we can learn from the corpse that lies before us. We look at this corpse. We say to ourselves: This corpse could never have come into being the way it is now. It is what remains of a human being whose soul and spirit were within it. The living person, the ensouled person, the spiritualized person must have existed beforehand in what lies before us as a corpse. Thus, we approach the reality of our thinking when we become aware of its deadness, and realize that it is the corpse of the living thinking that was in us before we descended into physical-sensory earthly existence.

Then the Guardian reminds us that our feeling is only half-alive, whereas our willing is fully alive, but we are only conscious of this externally.

The Guardian of the Threshold also reminds us that in order to gradually find the transition to living thinking, we should look up to the heavenly heights; that to grasp the nature of feeling we should look out to the cosmic reaches, and to gain an idea of the nature of will we should look to the world's depths, to the earthly depths.

But at the same time the Guardian shows us how we are placed with our thinking — when we look up to the cosmic thinking in which our earthly-physical thinking is rooted — between light and darkness; how the light can be dangerous if we devote ourselves unilaterally to it, how the darkness can be dangerous if we devote ourselves unilaterally to it, how we must seek our direction and goal in the middle between light and darkness if we are to find the truth, how we stand in the middle between warmth and cold with our feeling, and how we can vanish in the sensual embers of feeling if we surrender ourselves to the warmth, and on the other hand harden in the cold.

The Guardian of the Threshold indicates to us how we should walk in the middle between soul-warmth and soul-cold on the Christ-path. The Guardian of the Threshold indicates to us that when we seek willing in the earthly depths we find ourselves in the middle between life and death; how life would have us vanish in timidity; how death would have us cramped in nothingness; that we must find willing in the Middle Way. That, my dear sisters and brothers, is what the Middle Way is — as it has been described since ancient Mystery times — which the human being must tread if he wants to follow the path to the spirit.

The Guardian of the Threshold, before whom we stand as the earnest first representative of Michael, for the real leader of this School is Michael, gives us further guidance: how we can escape from this *apparent* thinking, from this dead thinking into the living essence of thinking. For this we must be prepared above all to strictly adhere to the laws which are prescribed for every esotericist in golden letters — he must only seize the gold — which the Guardian of the Threshold now repeats to us.

He makes us attentive to the yawning abyss of being before us, which we must fly over, because with earthly feet we cannot cross; how we will have then entered the spiritual world, for there on the other side of the yawning abyss deep, night-cloaked darkness is still before us. But we must enter beyond the yawning abyss of being into that deep, night-cloaked, cold darkness. Out of it warmth must come to us, out of it must come light which illumines our own Self, which warms our own Self. We cannot find the firm support-point in the spirit if, whenever we are over there, we do not remember the pledge that our soul makes, now that we are in this situation, after having received the previous admonitions from the Guardian of the Threshold, who now says:

Do not forget that as long as you are an earthly human being, even when you have crossed over to the spiritual world, that once you have returned you must adhere to the laws of the earth. When you enter the spiritual world with your thinking, you may not believe that when you return and organize your work and your thoughts in the earthly environment you may fly around dreaming within the earthly environment. You must reserve the flying for your thinking when you are in the spiritual world. You must practice deep, inner, intimate modesty, always wanting to be a man among men when you cross back to the ordinary world of ordinary consciousness. It is precisely by wishing to stay modest in the world, by abstaining from using the laws of the spiritual life in the ordinary world, that you will have the strength to grasp thinking in a way that it can serve you in spiritual worlds.

The Guardian of the Threshold therefore teaches us about thinking thus:

> You climb down to the earthly element
> With forces of your will unfolding;
> As thinker you bestride the earthly realm,
> Your animal-likeness will be shown
> To you by your own force of thought;
> The fear you feel of self you must
> Transform into courage of soul.

We must go through this by letting the mantric verse work on us. We must, if we wish to enter into the essential element of the earth, that means in the spiritual element of the earth; we must, my dear sisters and brothers, come to the point where we realize that our thinking is at first animal-like. We must experience fear of our own Self that is still animal-like; then the fear will give birth to its opposite and become the courage we need. That is the Guardian of the Threshold's urgently strong, earnest admonition, which cuts deeply into the heart. He admonishes us that we should feel this way when we tread the earth-element. We have already heard about treading the elements from the Guardian of the Threshold.

He admonishes us further: when, as feeling beings, we enter the fluid element, in the world of the water-beings, that we should not be aware of fear of our own Self, but we should be aware of how we sleep dreaming in this water element, which is our sculptor, as we have seen. And it is just when we become conscious that we live a plant-like existence in our earthly human feeling, that this feeling awakens us, for it shows us how lame our Self is. We will awaken once we have the humility to recognize the lameness of our Self.

Thirdly, when we feel ourselves to be in the air element with our willing — first in the earth-element with thinking, then in the water-element with feeling, then with willing in the air-element — then we will feel in this air-element that we have nothing in willing except what our normal memory gives us: memory-image-forms. We must seize these image-forms, which rest passively in our thoughts, with the will; then we are grasping the air-element in inner images. And our own soul will appear to us as if it were ossified. If we eliminate the earth and the air in thought and imagine ourselves wanting to breathe in the air-element, how ossified will we seem. But just by feeling this death by cold that we pass through, the spiritual fire will come to us, which we need in order to really grasp our willing.

The verses are profound, which the Guardian of the Threshold presents to our souls. Only if we observe them well and have fear of ourselves and know that we are nullified if we only perceive the earth in thought, will we have the courage in our souls for living thinking. When we sense how lame in feeling we are on earth, half living and lame, will the strength grow in us which allows us to awaken, so that we are awake in spiritual life, with the feeling we had before we descended to earthly physical existence. Then, when we have willingly descended into the air-element with our memory, we feel sclerotic and shivering with cold. But it is just when we feel this shivering from the cold the opposite happens, the spiritual fire awakens, showing us that our earthly willing is sleeping, but rooted in the living willing which was in us before we descended to earthly existence. We must learn to remember our existence before we descended to earthly existence.

In respect to feeling, the Guardian of the Threshold admonishes us:

> You live with the water-element
> Through feeling's weaving dream alone;
> To wake pervading water's being
> Will show the soul in you
> To be a sluggish plant-like being;
> But lameness of your Self
> Must Lead to self-awakening.

In respect to willing, the Guardian speaks:

> You sense in the waves of air
> The image-forms of memory only;
> Through willing to seize the essence of air,

Your own soul will threaten you
As coldly hardened stone;
But self-hood's death by cold,
It must give way to spirit-fire.

[The mantra is written on the blackboard with the corresponding underlining:]

The Guardian speaks with great earnestness:

You climb down to the earthly element
With forces of your will unfolding
As thinker you bestride the earthly realm,
Your animal-likeness will be shown
To you by your own force of thought
The fear you feel of self you must
Transform into courage of soul.

You live with the water-element
Through feeling's weaving dream alone;
To wake pervading water's being
Will show the soul in you
To be a sluggish plant-like being;
But lameness of your Self
Must Lead to self-awakening.

You sense in the waves of air
The image-forms of memory alone;
Through willing to seize the essence of air,
Your own soul will threaten you
As coldly hardened stone;
But self-hood's death by cold,
It must give way to spirit-fire.

We descend from thinking to feeling in memory when we let this verse work on us. And when we arrive at the depths of memory — where soul-life otherwise vanishes because the images of memory arise anew — there is the boundary, just as a mirror is a boundary. What comes to us from without arrives at something like a memory-wall, then it returns again and again. If one does not look behind the mirror, one does not see behind the memory-wall. But here the Guardian of the Threshold advises us that we must push through what is otherwise a boundary in order to enter the realm of spirit.

After the Guardian of the Threshold has referred us more to our interior with his admonishing verses and has left us time to process the contents of the verses in the soul — for when we use these mantric verses in meditation, we must allow ourselves a very long time, especially at this point, so they can work in us with their force and really bring our I downward through thinking, feeling and remembrance to what lies behind all remembrance — then the Guardian tells us how we should comport ourselves in respect to the outer world.

He draws our attention again up to the light, which however only lives in us in what *seem* to be thoughts. It is light that thinks in us. When the light pervades us, it thinks in us. But in earthly life light is only the appearance of a thinking that thinks itself. If we don't go beyond it, untrue spiritual being will lead us to the illusion of self-hood rather than to true self-hood So we must realize that if we only concentrate on thinking, we will wind up with the illusion of self-hood. But it is just this understanding of ourselves as earthly human beings, after having gone through the delusion of self-hood — through thinking, which, however, is capable of carrying us over the abyss of being to grasp the world's hardships and problems — that will enable us to gradually find support for experiencing existence in thought.

From light's shining force
Your thoughts you retain within;
When shining light in you itself does think,
Will then an untrue spirit-being cause
Illusion of self-hood to arise in you.
Reflecting on the needs of earth
Preserves your human state of being.

Now the Guardian of the Threshold teaches us how in feeling, at first, we only retain the wonderful, all-embracing forms of the world. But when we only retain these forms in feeling, our spiritual experience remains powerless. Self-hood suffocates if we always only stare, feeling, at what has been formed in the world. But if we begin to love all that is worthy in the world around us, we find being in feeling and we rescue our humanity.

The world's forms you only retain
In feelings held fast within;
When world-form feels itself in you,
The powerless experience of spirit
Will stifle in you the sense of self-hood;
But love of all that's worthy on earth
Will rescue for you your human soul.

Generally, we try to hatch thoughts from earthly values. We only retain the illusion of light if we don't consider the earth's weighty problems. We retain what is formed on the earth only in vague feelings if we don't experience this earthly interweaving of forms and gestalt with love.

And what can we retain of the world's life by willing? Our willing exists in the world's life. But if we only retain it by willing, we again fail to reach being. When the life of the world completely engulfs us, destructive spiritual exaltation kills the experience of Self. Immersion in the world's willing causes spiritual exaltation to erupt, which kills us. But if we develop the will in spiritual dedication to the higher worlds, if we think about what we are willing in the physical-sensory world in a way that the gods act in us, who inspire and give impulse to our willing, if we will in the service of the gods, then God lets his being give impulse to us as humans, and we sense real being in godly permeated willing.

You only retain of worldly life
The will within;
If worldly life takes hold in full,
Destructive spirit exaltation
Will kill experience of Self in you;
But spirit-dedicated earthly willing
Allows the God in man to reign.

These are the three admonitions which the Guardian of the Threshold calls out to us in the most earnest moments.

[The mantra is written on the blackboard:]

The Guardian speaks as though the Cosmic-Word itself were resounding:

From light's shining force
our thoughts you retain within;

— It is as though the Guardian wanted to bring our attention to what we are actually doing. He says that we have not yet gotten over forming mere thoughts about light's shining —

When shining light in you itself does think,
Will then an untrue spirit-being cause
Illusion of self-hood to arise in you.
Reflecting on the needs of earth
Preserves your human state of being

The world's forms you only retain
In feelings held fast within

— Once again, the admonition that in our vague, unfocused feelings only what is so wonderfully formed by the world is alive. At first the forming of the world is apprehended in the microcosm through the vagueness of feelings —

When world-form feels itself in you

— that is, not when we sense the world-form with our feelings, but when the world-form penetrates us, the macrocosm into the microcosm —

When world-form feels itself in you,
Experience of spirit is powerless,

— we become aware of our own powerlessness —

When world-form feels itself in you,
Experience of spirit is powerless,
And stifles in you the sense of self-hood;
But love of all that's worthy on earth
Will rescue for you your human soul.

We need this rescuing, for we are about to cross over the abyss. If we only carry over the thoughts instilled by the illusion of light, if we only carry over the vague feelings about world-form, then spiritual exaltation destroys the true light on the other side; powerless feeling, asleep, destroys the experience of the spiritual. We need awareness of the earth's needs, of all that the earth suffers, in order to be worthy to cross over to the spiritual world and not be destroyed by worldly thinking. We need love for what is worthy on the earth in order not to be turned to dust if we cross over with vague feelings. And thirdly, for willing we need this:

> *You only retain of worldly life*
> *The will within;*
> *If worldly Life takes hold in full,*

— and it will do so over there —

> *Destructive spirit exaltation*
> *Will kill experience of Self in you;*
> *But spirit-dedicated earthly willing*
> *Allows the God in man to reign.*

We may not merely carry over to the spiritual world what we have on this side. We must carry over a stronger soul than we have here. We must prepare the soul:

[As the following is spoken, the words between quotation marks are underlined on the blackboard:]

On the other side, we find "light's shining force". It lives in our thinking. We need "Reflecting on the needs of earth". Compassion for all the earth's suffering will preserve our "human state of being".

Over there, because we are coming to the World-formation, we don't only need our "feelings", we need "love for all that's worthy on earth"; then our "human soul" will be rescued. Here [in the first verse]: preserve our human state of being; here [in the second verse:] the human soul is rescued.

We must enter the full "worldly life", which in our "willing" is only a weak reflection, is too flimsy to pass over. And we must develop "spiritually developed earthly willing" for the "god in man" to reign.

This is the escalation:

> Light's shining force
> World-formation
> love for all that's worthy on earth
>
> > Thoughts
> > Feelings
> > Willing
>
> We need:
> Reflecting on the needs of earth,
> Love for all that's worthy on earth,
> Spiritually developed earthly willing;

for we need:
to preserve our human state of being,
to rescue the human soul,
to receive the reigning God within us.

That, my dear sisters and brothers, is what the Guardian places before our souls so that we may develop the wings of soul needed to cross over.

In the next esoteric lesson, to be held on Wednesday, it will be necessary that we receive the mantras through the Guardian of the Threshold — who in this case is Michael's representative at the threshold to the spiritual lands — the mantras which are the first that we speak when we arrive in the spiritual realm, which, however, appears before the human being when receiving these mantras as deep, night-cloaked, cold darkness.

Today, though, after this has been shown to our souls, let us again contemplate what speaks to us from all being, encouraging us toward all that the Guardian of the Threshold has placed before us with such firmness:

O man, know thyself!
So resounds the Cosmic-Word.
You hear it strong in soul,
You feel it firm in spirit.

Who speaks with such cosmic might?
Who speaks with such depth of heart?

Does it work through distant radiant space
Into your senses' sense of being?
Does it ring through weaving waves of time
Into your life's evolving stream?

It's you yourself who,
In feeling space, in experiencing time,

Create the Word, feeling foreign
In space's the soulless void
Because you lose the force of thought
In time's destroying flow.

And what has been placed before our souls by the Guardian of the Threshold's words is Michael's message in this rightfully established Michael School. If we receive them with the right attitude, Michael's being is present in this room, consecrating and strengthening what has been placed before our souls. Therefore, it may be accompanied by Michael's Sign. Michael's Sign is:

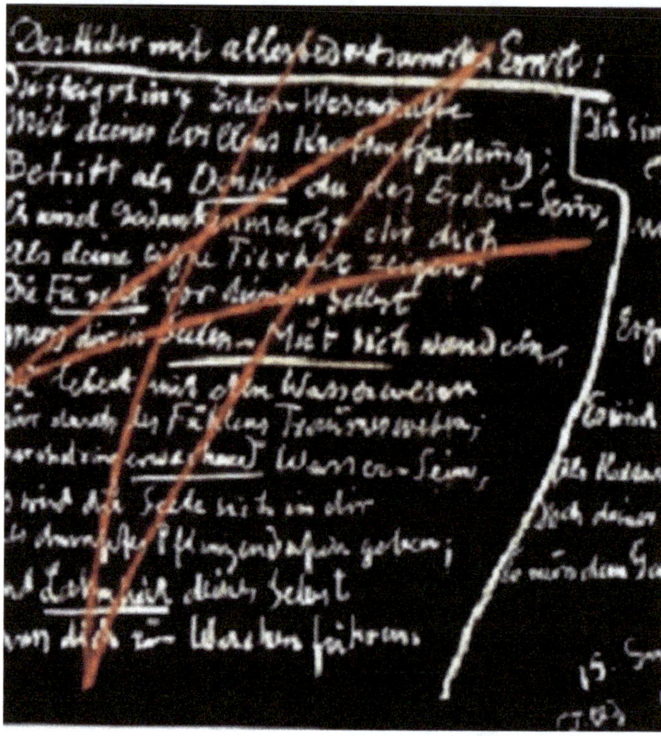

[in red]

and Michael's Seal, which he has impressed on the Rosicrucian mood for centuries, and which is expressed in the dictum:

> ex deo nascimur
>
> In Christo morimur
>
> Per spiritum sanctum reviviscimus

The first words, “I revere the Father”, are spoken accompanied by the gesture:

The second words, "I love the Son" are accompanied by the gesture:

The third words, "I unite myself with the Spirit", are accompanied by the gesture:

The first gesture means:

I revere the Father

the second gesture:

I love the Son

the third gesture.
I unite myself with the Spirit.

Thus, we may understand what is spoken as having been strengthened by Michael's sign and confirmed by Michael's Seal, which is thus, thus and thus, [indicating the Seal gestures on the blackboard] which is impressed over the Rosicrucian words.

So, should the verses live, which have been given through Michael's Sign, and sealed by the Michaelic Rosicrucian-School for your souls:

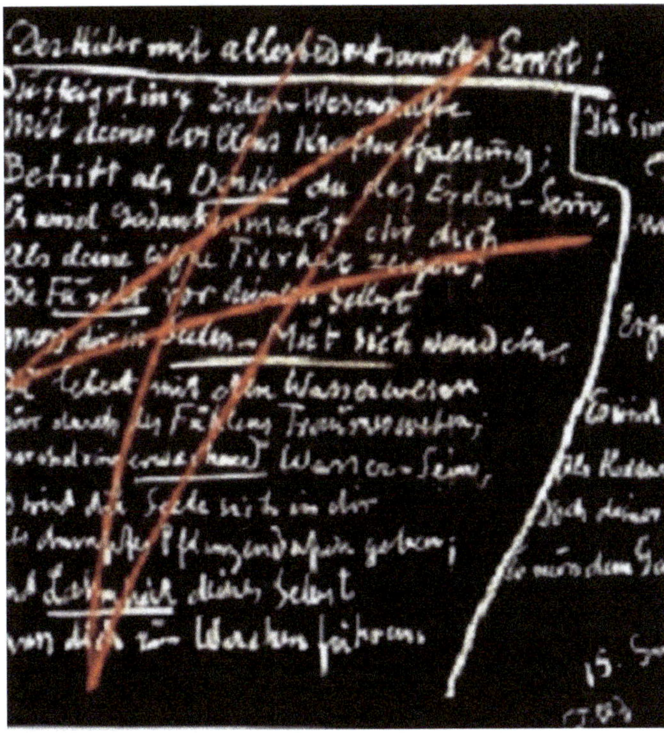

[Michael Sign]

The following is spoken, accompanied by the Seal Gestures:

ex deo nascimur

In Christo morimur

Per spiritum sanctum reviviscimus.

My dear sisters and brothers, the mantric verses which are given in this School may only be possessed by the School's rightful members, that is, those who have the blue membership certificate. Someone who could not be present at a lesson after the date of his admittance at which he could have been present, may receive the verses given after the date of his admittance from another member who has rightfully received them here in the School. For this it is necessary to obtain permission from either Dr. Wegman or myself.

This is not an administrative measure, but it is a basis of an occult school that a real action precedes something like this. Only the person who wants to give the verses to another may make the request to Dr. Wegman or to me, not the one who wants to receive them. Therefore, one can request the verses from another. But permission may not be requested by the one who is to receive the verses, but the one who is to give them. It would be useless for the recipient to ask.

Whoever copies something other than the mantras may keep it for a week; thereafter he is obliged to burn it, for what lives in this School should only live within the School and not outside it. This has nothing to do with power or arbitrary measures. It is all based on occult laws. Because if anything falls into the wrong hands, it loses its effectiveness for those for whom it is intended. If misuse prevails in that mantric verses or the contents of what is given here are given to the wrong people, the mantric verses and what is being given here lose their effectiveness for those who are present. These are facts, not some kind of arbitrary measures.

*

The program for tomorrow is: again at 9.30 the Pastoral Medicine lesson, at 12 o'clock the speech-formation course, at 5.30 the course for theologians and at 8 o'clock the lecture for members.

Lesson Six
(recapitulation)

Dornach, September 17, 1924

My dear sisters and brothers,

Once again, I must say that the introduction about the character and the responsibilities connected with the School cannot be repeated for the new arrivals each time. Therefore, I must request that those of you who were already here and have the mantras inform the new members concerning the contents of the introduction.

Today we will once again begin with the words which contain the fundamental exhortation to the human being, which resound to him from all the kingdoms of nature and from all the spiritual hierarchies, if he has the necessary sensibility, to seek his own being, and also exhort him to recognize, through his own being, the world in its true spiritual nature. They resound from all that interweaves and lives in the earthly depths, in water and air, in warmth and light, from what lives in the mountains and springs, in rocks, in the plants and animals, in the physical human form, in human souls, in human spirits, what lives in the residents of the stars, in the spiritual hierarchies — it resounds thus:

O man, know thyself!
So resounds the Cosmic-Word.
You hear it strong in soul,
You feel it firm in spirit.

Who speaks with such cosmic might?
Who speaks with such depth of heart?

Does it work through distant radiant space
Into your senses' sense of being?
Does it ring through weaving waves of time
Into your life's evolving stream?

It's you yourself who,
In feeling space, in experiencing time,
The Word create, feeling foreign
In space's soulless void,

Because you lose the force of thought
In time's destroying flow.

My dear sisters and brothers, the description of the spiritual path which leads from the sunny, light-filled world in which we live on earth appears on the other side of the yawning abyss of being at first as a gloomy, night-cloaked darkness. The path which leads us to where we become aware that, when we seek our own being in all that lives in the depths, flows in the air, all that creeps and flies, in all that our senses perceive in the majestic glow of the stars, in the powerful depths of universal space, in the immeasurably distant flow of time, that all that does not contain our being, the true source of our humanity, that it becomes gloomy when we look here for our humanity. The description has led us thus far to show that we must find the way past the Guardian of the Threshold, who has told us so much about the meaning of the spiritual world, over to what is still night-cloaked, black gloom, so that it can become bright there, and in this brightness the light arises to illumine before the eyes of our soul our own being, and therewith the being and essence and interweaving of the world.

It must be clear to us that in the moment — and we have come so far in the description — when we have crossed over the abyss of being, past the Guardian of the Threshold, in that moment an important change takes place in the human being, that is, in ourselves.

Let us look, my dear sisters and brothers, at our human existence as it is between birth and death on earth: we grasp the world thinking, we grasp the world feeling, we act in the world by willing. But thinking, feeling and willing are interwoven in our human earthly existence. If we want to carry out something in the near future, we consider it first, so what we carry out is already present as a seed in our thoughts. We see it flowing out in impulses of will. We feel that it is worthy. We feel love flowing to this or that being. Because we feel it, we form a thought about it. Or we go beyond that and carry out a deed of love towards the being, we let ourselves grow wings of love, and are urged forward to willing. But all that — thinking, feeling, willing — is closely related to our humanity as it unfolds between birth and death in the physical world. We are at one in thinking, feeling and willing.

And the truth is that we are only really awake in our thoughts. They are bright and clear, although the Guardian of the Threshold had revealed them to be illusory. They are bright and clear, we are awake in them.

Our feeling is darker and less clear. We are closer to existence in feeling, but the content of what we feel is like a dream, so that we can only speak of dream-feeling, even when awake.

The will, however, as it emerges from our being, remains at first completely unclear to our normal consciousness. We have the thought that we want this or that; the thought appears, grasps the organism; the organism acts, carries out the thought; we see what we have carried out, again with thought. But the will itself rests in deep sleep, as do the things in our soul rest between falling asleep and awakening.

But the initiate sees the thoughts in their living state, which they were in before the human being had descended from the supersensible world to the sensory one. He sees radiant being in the thoughts. But this radiant being he sees is not the illusion of thoughts as in ordinary thinking.

We stand beside the Guardian of the Threshold. The abyss of being is there; before us — beyond the abyss, beyond the threshold — is the black, night-cloaked gloom; but from out of the darkness gleaming, living shapes are moving. We say to ourselves — because we sense that the kind of thoughts we had as physical persons have abandoned us — we say to ourselves: There is our flowing, living thinking. It doesn't belong to us now, it belongs to the world. Light on light, thought extracts itself from the black gloom. We know that thought, all our thinking, is there as the first brightness within the black gloom that we are approaching.

And then we see something further down. We have the feeling — and the Guardian of the Threshold points to it with an admonishing gesture — we see how the darkness below is becoming fire-like. Fire, dark fire yes, but fire that we can sense psychically, spreads out below us. What we recognize as our willing comes towards us over the abyss of being. The initiate gradually learns the following: What happens when thinking merges with willing? The thought — of what is wanted — is grasped; then this thought merges with corporeality as beneficent fire. What brings the will to existence is warmth, which is fire when our own will meets us from out of the darkness.

And between this warmth, from which our willing streams toward us across the abyss of being (for our human will is a mere reflection of our cosmic will) — between this warm, dark out-streaming from below, which has at most a whiff of bluish-violet, and the bright lights of thoughts above, between both there is an interweaving, flowing warmth rising, light descending. Light-enveloped warmth rising, warmth-enveloped light streaming down: that is our feeling.

It is a powerful picture which the Guardian of the Threshold draws. And now we know that when we cross over from the sensory world, from the world of physical reality in which we are between birth and death, into the world of the spirit, then we will be — in thinking, feeling and willing — no longer the unity that we are here; there we are Three. In the universe, we are Three: our thinking merges with light across the threshold; our will becomes fire; our feeling becomes light-enveloped fire.

We must have the courage to expand and intensify the Self, the I, so that it holds the Three together when we cross over. We can do this once we are permeated with what could otherwise be a banality: that our head is the source of all our senses and thinking: All our senses and thoughts are distributed over the whole body, but what is especially expressed in our head is that in its roundness, with an opening below, it imitates the shape of the universe. If we can say to ourselves in all seriousness and inner ardency: my head is inwardly and outwardly an imitation of the world's shape, we feel then, in that we want to view the head from within, how this perspective expands to include the universe, which is only concentrated in our head for our earthly vision.

We should then intensely feel how our heart, the physical expression of our soul, does not only beat because of what is in our body, because of what is enclosed within the skin; we breathe in the air, which is the impetus of the heartbeat, we breathe it out again. The world in all its grandeur and majesty participates in our heartbeat. What is sensed in our heart is not merely what is within us: it is the universal pulse-beat.

If we consider how our limbs work through willing, it gives us the strength to not only will what is within us. Consider for a moment how the forces of heredity are in us when we are born, how the forces of karma, which we have acquired through many, many earth-lives, live in our willing. Let us think of all that, and feel: when we will, world-force lives in our limbs, not merely human force.

Just think, my dear sisters and brothers, while still here at the Guardian of the Threshold's side he points over to the brightly lit, universally living and acting thoughts; to what wells up as warmth, light-bringing, light-filled; to what spiritually wafts over us from below like warm wind — the universe's fire, which is the ur-force of the will.

So we hear, resounding, what the Guardian of the Threshold has to say to us in this situation:

Behold the Three

(thinking, feeling, willing; man is split in three)

Behold the Three,
They are the One,
When you in earthly life
the human imprint bear.

Experience the head's cosmic form

The Guardian makes this sign:

[It is drawn on the blackboard.]

so that we stop and feel the head's cosmic form in this closed, upward pointing triangle. Let us concentrate on this.

Feel the heart's cosmic beat

The Guardian makes this sign:

[It is drawn on the blackboard.]

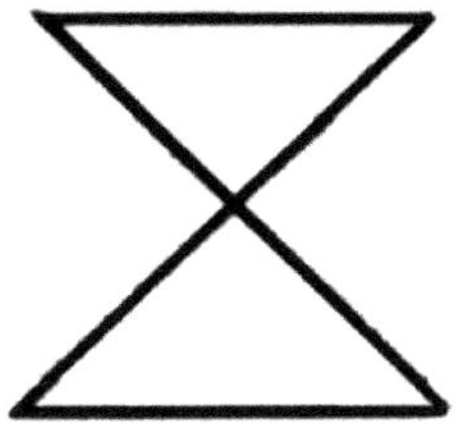

for us to feel in this sign the wave-like pulse of the universe, which crosses in the heart.

Consider the cosmic force of the limbs.

The Guardian of the Threshold makes the other sign:

[It is drawn on the blackboard:]

We should concentrate on this line in order to sense the mantric force of this line and of the whole verse.

Then the Guardian of the Threshold strengthens it again:

> They are the Three,
> The Three, which as the One
> In earthly being live.

This is the verse by which the Guardian announces how we are to prepare — through forceful courage, through ardent striving for knowledge — to sense the wings which carry us over from the One to the Three. In the physical world, we are the One. In the spiritual world, we are the Three, which we experience in imaginative pictures.

[Written on the blackboard]

The Guardian reminds us:

See the Three,
They are the One,
When you in earthly life
The human imprint bear.

[Alongside the first sign on the blackboard is written:]

<u>Experience</u> the head's cosmic <u>shape</u>
the cosmic shape can be experienced in the head

[Alongside the second sign is written:]

<u>Sense</u> the heart's cosmic <u>beat</u>
the cosmic beat can be sensed in the heart

[Alongside the third sign is written:]

<u>Consider</u> the limbs' cosmic <u>force</u>
the cosmic force can be considered in the movement of the limbs.

The escalation is:

[The following words are underlined:]

<u>Experience</u>
<u>Sense</u>
<u>Consider</u>

<u>Shape</u>
<u>Beat</u>
<u>Force</u>

The three lines must be strengthened by concentrating on these figures.

[Written:]

They are the Three,
The Three, which as the One
In earthly being live.

My dear friends, when we are standing here in earthly existence — and we are still doing so, we are just preparing to cross to the spiritual world — we ascribe to our head our spirit, in that it contains thoughts. At first, though, this spirit is only apparent. The thoughts are the appearance of the spirit. We ascribe the thoughts to our head, that is, we ascribe the spirit to our head, because the spirit lives in the form of thoughts during earthly existence.

But we can do something else, recalling the Guardian of the Threshold's admonition. In this situation, as we are preparing to cross over the abyss of being, we must endeavor to concentrate on the force we normally use when we move a limb, when we walk or stand, when our will pervades us. We must endeavor to concentrate to the extent that we will each thought, as though it were being pushed out. We must sense the thought being pushed out as when we stretch out an arm: thus, reality passes through the will into the thoughts. Then the things perceived by our senses, whereas they came to us previously as the appearance of color or tone, now stream toward us from the multifaceted sensory appearance as cosmic will.

My dear sisters and brothers: Learn to extend your thoughts out to the world as you learn to stretch out your hands through willing. Just as the objects of the world respond when you extend your will to them, offering resistance, so do the spirits offer resistance when you extend your thoughts to them, in that the will permeates them. If we do this, we are interweaving reality in wisdom. The Guardian of the Threshold's admonishes us once again.

The Guardian's last admonition:

The head's spirit,
You can will it;

(otherwise we only think it, now we will it; and when we do so, willing becomes something different)

And willing

(the willing of thoughts)

provides you with
The senses' multi-forming heaven-weave;
You interweave with wisdom.

The next thing the Guardian of the Threshold points to is the heart, in which the rhythm of our humanity is concentrated. We cannot bring anything except feeling into the heart, that is, feeling here in the sensory world between birth and death. But we must also bring the feelings to the heart when we are in the spiritual world.

If we could feel the heart as if the world were feeling our heart, because we are, after all, in the world, then our feeling would be different. Just as willing becomes "the senses' multi-forming heaven-weave", so feeling becomes something which must be conceived of in a way that we can say — Look: thinking, the spirit's head, becomes the will; feeling remains feeling, but rays out to thinking on one side and willing on the other. It is both at the same time. Therefore, at this point we must get used to concentrating on a line in which we interweave what rays upward and downward.

This line must read as follows: "And feeling becomes your will's thinking, your thinking's will, the awakening seed of cosmic life." Then you live in the glow. This is not a dying away glow, it is the world's revelation in beauty, which can also be called "glow" in the sense of "gloria". The glow here means gloria.

Thus, the Guardian's second admonition is:

The heart's soul,
You can feel it;
And feeling becomes for you
The awakening seed of cosmic life:
  Will's thinking, thinking's will.
    You live in the glow.

[This second verse is written on the blackboard and "heart's" and "feeling" are underlined:]

The heart's soul,
You can feel it;
And feeling becomes for you
The awakening seed of cosmic life:
  Will's thinking, thinking's will.
    You live in the glow.

You must, my dear sisters and brothers, by practicing this, try to think that — the will's thinking, the thinking's will — flow together in one, because it is so in the world.

The third thing to which the Guardian of the Threshold points is the force of our limbs. The Guardian of the Threshold demands that that our spirit wills our limbs, that we do not feel that what we do is the result of exerting our own force, but that we observe it as if we stepped out of our bodies and were standing beside ourselves. Then the will's thinking becomes the thinking which we unfold here: the will's goal-oriented human striving. And now we recognize the virtue of human diligence, what human will can accomplish in the world's evolution. The guardian of the Threshold admonishes us:

[The third verse is written on the blackboard and "limbs" is underlined.]

The limbs' force,
You can think it
And thinking becomes

The will's goal-oriented human striving.
You strive in virtue.

The escalation is:

[Now the following three words are underlined:]

<u>weave</u>
<u>live</u>
<u>strive</u>.

The other escalation is:

wisdom
glow
virtue.

Now I will read the lines as the appear to us at first when the Guardian speaks them to us:

The head's spirit,
You can will it;
And willing becomes for you
The senses' multi-formed heaven's interweaving.
You interweave in wisdom.

The heart's soul,
You can feel it;
And feeling becomes for you
The will's thinking, thinking will´s
Awakening seed of cosmic life.
You live in the glow.

The limbs' force,
You can think it;
And thinking becomes
The will's goal-oriented human striving.
You strive in virtue.

That is the Guardian of the Threshold's last admonition.

That is the decisive point which is indicated by the words which are spoken here as the words Michael himself speaks, because this Esoteric School has been founded and is sustained by Michael and his force. Now we have come to the important point in our instruction where, if we have conscientiously practiced all that we have learned, it gives us wings to fly over the yawning, deep abyss of being.

Everything which has been said in this Michael School shall again be accompanied by the sign and seals of Michael; for all has been given in such a way that while it resounds through the space of this School, Michael is present, which may be confirmed by his sign:

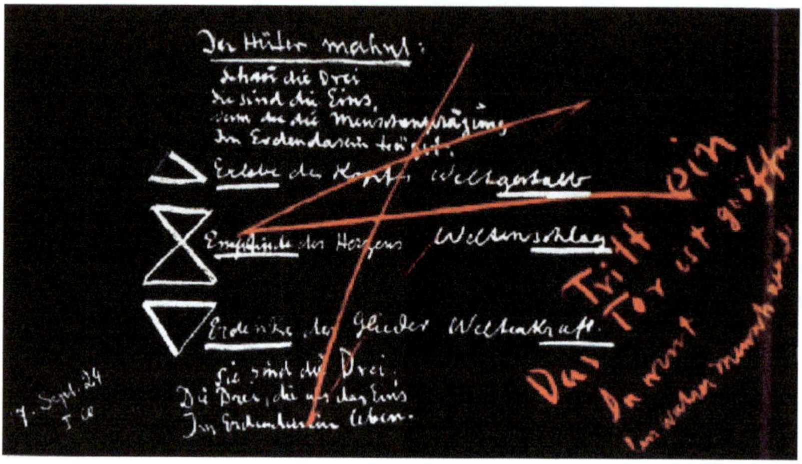

[Michael-sign (in red)
Come in, the door has opened, you will become a free human being]

and which may be confirmed by his seal, which he has impressed on the threefold Rosicrucian verse:

Ex deo nascimur

In Christo morimur

Per spiritum sanctum reviviscimus

the seal makes us feel the first line in this gesture:

[The lower seal is drawn on the blackboard.]

[lower seal-gesture]

the second line in this gesture:

[the middle seal gesture is drawn on the blackboard]

[middle seal gesture]

the third verse in this gesture:

[the upper seal gesture is drawn on the blackboard]

[upper seal-gesture]

As we know, this first gesture means [beside the lower gesture is written:]

I revere the Father

We feel this as we say "Ex deo nascimur" and confirm it by the gesture, which is Michael's seal.

The second gesture means [beside the second gesture is written:]

I love the Son

We feel this while saying "In Christo morimur", thus expressing the feeling through what lies in the Michael-Seal.

The third gesture means:

I unite with the spirit

It accompanies, in feeling, "Per spiritum sanctum reviviscimus." It is the gesture which is Michael's seal upon the third part of the Rosicrucian verse.

Thus, Michael's Sign and Seal accompany the path onward, which will be followed in this School for spiritual development:

[the Michael-Sign is made]

[The following three lines are spoken, accompanied by the three seal-gestures:

Ex deo nascimur

In Christo morimur

Per spiritum sanctum reviviscimus.

Then the moment comes when the Guardian of the Threshold's decisive words resound as though coming from Michael, as though from the cosmic distances. After the Guardian has said how we are to prepare ourselves — and we feel this preparation to be necessary — then his words resound as though coming from Michael, as though coming from the cosmic distances:

Come in.
The door has opened.
You will become
A true human being.

We must create the feeling that we are not speaking ourselves, but that as we are speaking it becomes objective, that we hear it, as if it is coming from the other side:

[Across the mantra "See the three" on the blackboard, the following is written in red chalk:]

Come in.
The door has opened.
You will become
A true human being.

In the following lessons, what resounds on the other side of the threshold will be described.

But now let us again consider — for all real development always leads back to the starting point — how from all the beings of the world the challenge speaks to us about what we have learned from the Guardian's mouth:

O man, know thyself!
So resounds the Cosmic-Word.
You hear it strong in soul,
You feel it firm in spirit.

Who speaks with such cosmic might?
Who speaks with such depth of heart?

Does it work through distant radiant space
Into your senses' sense of being?
Does it ring through weaving waves of time
Into your life's evolving stream?

It's you yourself who,
In feeling space, in experiencing time,

The Word create, feeling foreign
In space's soulless void,
Because you lose the force of thought
In time's destroying flow.

Once more — confirming all, confirming Michael's presence — the sign and seal of Michael:

[the Michael-sign is made]

[The following is spoken together with the seal-gestures:]

Ex deo nascimur

In Christo morimur

Per spiritum sanctum reviviscimus.

The mantric verses given here in order to practice contain the force necessary to experience what is described here. Only the members of this Class may possess them, no one else. If someone who belongs to the School cannot attend a lesson during which he would have received the corresponding verse, he may receive it from another member who was present. But for each time this happens permission must be received either from Dr. Wegman or myself. However, the one who is to receive the verse may not request permission, but only the one who is to give it.

Once permission has been granted to give someone the verses, it continues to hold good for that particular person. For every other person, permission must be obtained from Dr. Wegman or myself. It would be useless for the one who wants to receive the verses to request permission; only the one who is to give them should ask. So, if one wants to have the verses, he must go to someone who has them legitimately. The latter should then ask for each individual to whom he wishes to give them.

If someone makes notes of something else, other than the verses, he is only authorized to keep them for one week; after that they must be burned. We must really observe the occult rules. An occult rule is contained in all I have said and insist upon. This is not an arbitrary administrative measure, but because if esoteric things fall into the wrong hands, then, my dear sisters and brothers, the mantras lose their force. It is simply based on an occult law.

*

At twelve o'clock tomorrow is the Speech Formation course; at 10.45 the Theology course; at five o'clock the Pastoral Medicine course and at eight o'clock the lecture for members.

Lesson Seven (recapitulation)

Dornach, September 20, 1924

My dear Sisters and Brothers,

Since the Christmas Conference an esoteric breath flows through the whole Anthroposophical Society. And those members of the Anthroposophical Society who have taken part in the general members' lectures will have noted how this esoteric breath flows through all the work within the anthroposophical movement now, and should do so in the future.

This was a necessity which, above all, flows from the spiritual world, from where the revelations come which should live in the anthroposophical movement.

Therefore, the necessity arose to create a certain nucleus for anthroposophical esoteric life, to create real esoteric life, and therewith the necessity arose to build a bridge to the spiritual world itself.

In a certain sense the spiritual world had to manifest the will for the creation of such a School. For an esoteric school cannot be created by human arbitrariness, nor from that human arbitrariness called "human ideals"; rather must this esoteric school be the body for something which flows out of spiritual life, so that everything that occurs in such a school presents the outer expression of an activity which in reality occurs in the spiritual world itself. Therefore, this esoteric school could not have been created without first asking the will of Michael, which since the last third of the nineteenth century has been guiding human affairs - something which I have often mentioned here in members' lectures.

In the course of time this will of Michael again and again cyclically intervenes in human affairs from the spiritual world. And when we look back in the evolution of time, we find that this same Michael-Will - which we can also call the Michael Reign - was active in the spiritual affairs of humanity, in the great questions of civilization before the Mystery of Golgotha, in the time of Alexander in Greece through the Chthonian and Celestial mysteries, and which was to spread to Asia and Africa. Where the Michael-Will reigns, there is always cosmopolitanism. What differentiates people on earth is overcome during the Michael age.

The most important influence, related to Aristotle and to Alexander, which was under the impulse of Michael, was followed by that of Oriphiel, and after Oriphiel came the Anael impulse, the Zachariel impulse, then the Raphael impulse, then the Samael impulse, then the Gabriel impulse, which extended into the 19th century. And since the seventies of the nineteenth century we are again under the sign of Michael's reign. It is in its beginnings. But Michael's impulses must flow into all legitimate esoteric activities in a conscious manner - what can be clear to you, my sisters and brothers, through the general lectures for members.

And everything connected with the Christmas Conference leads to what is constituted as the basis of the anthroposophical movement's formation of this Esoteric School inspired and guided by Michael. It therefore rightfully exists in our times as a spiritual institution. All those who want to be rightful members of this School must accept this in their lives with the deepest sincerity. They must feel that they don't merely belong to an earthly community, but to a supersensible community, whose guide and leader is Michael himself. Therefore, everything communicated here is not to be understood as my words, insofar as they are the content of the lessons, but rather as what Michael communicates in an esoteric manner to those who feel they belong with him in this age. Therefore, what these lessons contain will be Michael's message for our age.

And it is because of this that the anthroposophical movement will receive its true spiritual strength. For this it is necessary that what membership in this School means be taken with the utmost earnestness. It is really necessary, my dear sisters and brothers, truly and deeply necessary, that it be indicated in the utmost earnest manner the sacred earnestness with which the School must be taken.

And here within the School it must be repeatedly said: in anthroposophical circles there is much too little earnestness for what really flows through the anthroposophical movement, and at least the esoteric members of the Esoteric School must be in the forefront of what humanity can gradually develop as the necessary earnestness. Therefore, it is necessary that the leadership of the School retain for itself the right to allow only those to enter as rightful, worthy members of the School who, in every aspect of their lives, want to be worthy representatives of anthroposophy; and the decision about whether this is the case or not must lie with the School's leadership.

Do not consider this, my sisters and brothers, as a limitation of freedom. The School's leadership must also have its freedom and be able to recognize who belongs to the School and who does not, just as each one is free to decide whether to belong to the School or not. So, a free, ideal-spiritual contract, so to speak, between each member of the School and the leadership must be agreed upon. In no other way could esoteric development be called healthy, especially not one which is worthy of the fact that this Esoteric School exists under the direct force of the Michael impulse itself.

Conscientious care of the mantric verses so that they do not fall into unauthorized hands is the first requisite; but also, to really be a worthy representative of the anthroposophical cause.

I only need to mention a few things to show how little the anthroposophical movement is still grasped with complete earnestness. It has happened that members of the School have reserved their seats by placing on them the blue membership certificates, which gives them the right to participate in the School. [1] It has happened in the Anthroposophical Society that whole piles of the News Sheets, only intended for members, have been found on the trolley cars that run from Dornach to Basel. And I could add many other examples to this list. And amazing things happen as a result of this lack of earnestness. Even with things that in everyday life are taken seriously, at the moment when those within the anthroposophical movement are expected to do so, they do not take them seriously.

These are things which must be considered in connection with the firm structure that this School must have. Therefore, these things must be said, because if they are not observed, one cannot worthily receive what is given here in the School as revelations from the spiritual world. At the end of each lesson, your attention is expressly drawn to the fact that the being of Michael is present while the revelations from the spiritual world are given, and are confirmed by Michael's sign and seal.

All these things must live in the members' hearts. And worthiness, profound worthiness must reign in all that is bound even in thought to the School. For only in this way what today is to be carried through the world as an esoteric stream can live. And that includes the duties incumbent on each individual.

The mantric verses written here on the blackboard can only be possessed, in the strictest sense of the word, by those who have the right to be present. And if a member of the School is unable to attend a lesson during which mantric verses are given, another member, who has the verses, may give them to him; but it must be for each individual case, that is, for each person to whom the verses are to be given, that permission must be requested, either from Dr. Wegman or from me. Once permission is granted in respect to a person, it remains valid. But permission must again be requested for each other individual. This is not an administrative rule, it is an occult rule that must be strictly adhered to. For every act of the School must be connected to the School's leadership: and that begins with having to request permission from the School's leadership for acts having to do with the School. Not the one who is to receive the mantras may ask, but only the one who is to give them, using the modality that I have just described. If someone takes notes on what is said here, except for the mantras, he is obliged to keep them for only one week, and then to burn them.

All these things are not arbitrary rules, but they relate to the occult fact that esoteric matters are only effective if they are embraced by the School members' attitude. The mantras lose their effectiveness if they fall into the wrong hands. And it is a rule so firmly inscribed in the cosmic order, that the following once happened and a whole group of mantras, which had been in effect within the anthroposophical movement, have been rendered ineffective.

I was able to give mantric verses to a number of people; I also gave them to a certain person, who had a friend. The friend was somewhat clairvoyant. And it happened that while the two friends were sleeping in the same room, the clairvoyant friend, when the other one merely repeated the mantra in thought, surreptitiously copied it and then did mischief with it by giving it to others as coming from himself. It was necessary to look into the matter, which revealed why the mantra became ineffective for all those who possessed it.

Therefore, my dear sisters and brothers, you must not take these things lightly, for esoteric rules are strict; and when someone has made such an error, he should not excuse himself by claiming that he was unable to avoid it. Of course, if someone runs through a mantra in his mind, and someone else copies it clairvoyantly, he certainly can do nothing about it. Nevertheless, the rules are applied with an iron necessity. [2]

I mention this so that you can see how little arbitrariness is involved, and how these things are being read from the spiritual world and that the practices of the spiritual world apply. Nothing is arbitrary in what occurs in a rightly existing esoteric school. And the earnestness from this esoteric school should stream out to the whole anthroposophical movement. For only then will this School be what it should be for the anthroposophical movement. But when something is done which only springs from personal motives and then it is pretended that it is because of devotion to the anthroposophical movement - well, I don't mean to say that it should not happen, because obviously, people today must be personal - but then it is also necessary that truth lives in what is personal, that for instance if someone comes here to Dornach for personal pleasure he should admit it and not pretend otherwise. There's nothing wrong with coming to Dornach for personal pleasure, in fact it is good. But one should admit it and not sidestep it by declaring pure dedication to spiritual life.

I mention this; I could just as well mention another example, which is more real, for it is really the case that when most of our friends come to Dornach, a will to sacrifice is involved, and that only in the least of cases is untruthfulness involved. But I've chosen this example because it is the least applicable and thus the least harmful. If I had mentioned other examples, what I would like to have as a calm prevailing mood in the hearts and souls of all who are sitting here now could not exist in the necessary degree.

After that introduction, I would like to start with the verse that is the beginning and end of Michael's proclamation to all unbiased human beings, and which contains what all entities in the world are saying, if one listens to them with the soul. For from all that lives in the mineral, vegetable and animal kingdoms, what sparkles down from the stars, what acts into our souls from the domains of the hierarchies, from all that crawls under and on the earth as worm-life, from what speaks in rocks and springs and fields and thunder and clouds and lightning; all these spoke to unbiased human beings in the past, speak at the present and will speak in the future:

O man, know thyself!
So resounds the Cosmic-Word.
You hear it strong in soul,
You feel it firm in spirit.

Who speaks with such cosmic might?
Who speaks with such depth of heart?

Does it work through distant radiant space
Into your senses' sense of being?
Does it ring through weaving waves of time
Into your life's evolving stream?

It's you yourself who,
In feeling space, in experiencing time,
The Word create, feeling foreign
In space's soulless void,
Because you lose the force of thought
In time's destroying flow.

The previous lesson ended, my dear sisters and brothers, with the Guardian of the Threshold giving the last admonitions before one passes over the yawning abyss of being; the Guardian of the Threshold spoke the weighty, moving words:

Come in,
The gate has opened;
You will become
A true human being.

Our souls and hearts have been exposed to the important, weighty, meaningful words spoken by the Guardian of the Threshold on behalf of Michael. And everything he said was to prepare us for the attitude we must have when we come over after the gate has been opened - over the yawning abyss of being, where one does not come walking with earthly feet, where one flies with the spiritual wings that grow when the soul is imbued with a spiritual attitude, with spiritual love, with spiritual feeling.

And now, now, my dear sisters and brothers, will be described what the human being experiences when he stands on the other side of the yawning abyss of being. The Guardian of the Threshold indicates to him: turn around and look back! Until now you have been looking at what appeared to you as black, night-cloaked gloom, about which you had to say that it will become inner light and will illumine your own Self. With the last admonitions — the Guardian of the Threshold says — I let it become lighter, at first most gently. You feel now the first light around you. But turn around, look back!

And now, when he who has crossed over the yawning abyss of being and turns around and looks back, he sees himself as an earthly human being, what he is during his physical incarnation, over there in the part of his being that he has left behind and which now lies in the earthly sphere. He observes his own human self there. He has embodied himself in spiritual being with his spirit-soul. The earthly environment is over there now. He stands there in the region, in which we first were with all our humanity, where we saw what crawls beneath and flies above, where we saw the sparkling stars, the warmth-giving sun, where we saw what lives in the wind and weather, and where, knowing that despite all its majesty, how the sun blazes and illumines, despite all the beauty and greatness accessible to the senses, we said to ourselves: our own humanity is not here; we must seek it on the other side of the yawning abyss of being, in what seems at first, to the senses, to be black, night-cloaked gloom.

The Guardian of the Threshold has shown, by the three beasts, what we actually are. Now will be described how in the gloom that is beginning to be light, we should begin to look back on what we as humans are in the sensory world, together with what was our only world in sensory earthly existence.

And now the Guardian of the Threshold points directly back there to the earthly man, which we ourselves also are during earthly existence, and to which we must continually return, into which we must always penetrate when we leave the spiritual world and return to our earthly duty. For we may not become dreamers and go into raptures, we must return completely to earth life. Therefore the Guardian of the Threshold directs us to look at the person who stands over there, who we ourselves are, in a way that at first draws our attention to what this person is. [An outline of a human being is drawn on the blackboard.]

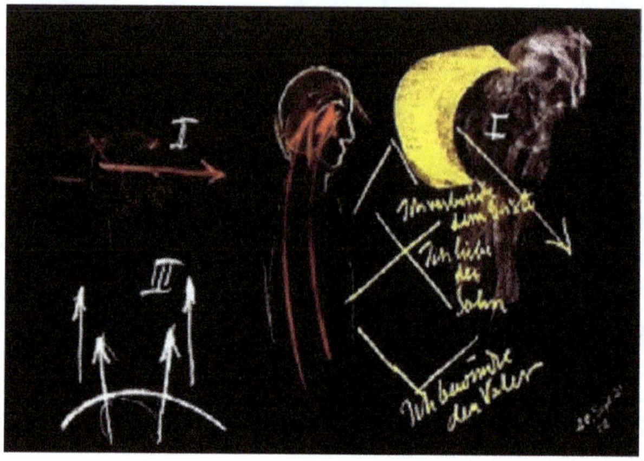

He knows that he perceives the outer world through the senses, which are mostly situated in the head, and that he perceives his thinking through the impulse of the head.

But the Guardian of the Threshold now says: Look into this head. It is like looking into a dark cell, for you do not see the creative light within it. The truth is that what you had as thinking over there in the sensory world is mere seeming, mere images, not much more than mirror-images.

The Guardian of the Threshold admonishes us to be very aware of this, but also to be aware that what is only appearance in earthly thinking is the corpse - as we have heard in previous lessons - of a living thinking in which we were immersed in the soul-spiritual world before we descended to this earthly life. There thinking lived! Now thinking rests as dead thinking, as seeming thinking in the coffin of our bodies. And all the thinking we use in the sensory world is dead thinking. It was alive before we descended.

And what has this thinking accomplished? It has created everything that is within the head, within this dark cell - as it appears to the senses - that is light-creating essence. The brain, which rests within as thinking's support, has been created by living thinking. [The interior of the head, yellow, is drawn on the blackboard.] It is living thinking that creates the support for our earthly semblance of thinking.

Observe the brain's convolutions, observe what you carry within the dark cell that enables you to think, my sisters and brothers, observe the semblance of thinking in the dark cell, then you will find in what is felt above as thinking [drawing: red arrows] from out of which streams the force of will into thinking, so that each thought is streamed through with will. How the will streams into thinking can be sensed.

And now we look back from the other side of the threshold at how that other person, who we ourselves are, has waves of will streaming out of his body into the head, which create the will, and finally, when we follow them back to the turning points of time which lead to our previous incarnations, how they create the waves of thought from worlds past into our present incarnation and form our heads, all of which makes the semblance of thinking in this incarnation possible.

Therefore, we must be strong, the Guardian of the Threshold tells us, and imagine dead thinking being cast out into the cosmic nothingness, for it is only seeming. And the willing that then arises we should consider as what comes over from previous incarnations and interweaves and works, making us thinkers. Within [drawing: yellow] are the creating cosmic thoughts. These creating cosmic thoughts enable us to have human thoughts.

Therefore, the first words the Guardian of the Threshold speaks after he has let us cross the threshold, and after he has announced that the gate has opened, that we can become true human beings, the first words he speaks are:

See behind thinking's sensory light,
How in the gloomy spirit-cell
Willing arises from the body's depths;
Let be cast, through your strength of soul,
Dead thinking into the cosmic void;
And willing, it will arise
As cosmic thought's creation.

The first words we hear on the other side, as we look back at the figure, which we ourselves are:

[The first mantra is written on the blackboard, together with a heading. Blackboard writing is always in italics.]

The Guardian is heard in the brightening darkness:

I

See behind thinking's sensory light,
How in the gloomy spirit-cell
Willing arises from the body's depths;
Let be cast, through your strength of soul,
Dead thinking into the cosmic void;
And willing, it will arise
As cosmic thought's creation.

And then the Guardian of the Threshold adds - and one must strain to hear him: Now imagine that you are observing that figure on the other side who you yourself are; you turn around again and look into the darkness and try with all your inner imaginative force of remembrance - as one does when retaining a physical after-image in the eye. Try with all your strength to draw before you something like a gray outline of what you saw over there, but avoid drawing anything except the outline of the figure. [It is drawn.]

Then, if one succeeds in seeing this gray outline of a figure, behind it appears an image of the moon [a sickle moon, yellow, is drawn], the gray figure before it.

If one is able to keep inner calm, one sees the moon in the distance. The gray figure outline is also there, but it is active in us. And if we practice this over and over, we feel we have arrived at the spiritual figure of the head that we had over there, not the physical human figure, but at the spiritual figure of the head that we had over there, if we can feel what karma brings to us from previous earthly incarnations. [yellow arrow at the right of the sickle moon.]

Therefore, you should meditate on this picture that I have drawn here, the sickle moon with this arrow; let the mantra unfold, with this picture as the marker for the gradual familiarization with what forcefully comes over from previous earthly existences.

And secondly, the Guardian of the Threshold points with a stronger gesture to what feeling is to the person over there, who we ourselves are, and he admonishes that we are to see this feeling as a dim dream. In fact, we see feeling - which makes the person over there more real than thinking, for thinking is illusion, whereas feeling is half reality - we see the person's feeling enfold in numerous dream-pictures during the day. We learn by observing it that feeling, for the spirit and in the spirit, is dreaming.

But what kind of dreaming is feeling? In this feeling, not only the individual dreams, but within it the whole surrounding world dreams. Our thinking is our own. That's why it's illusion. The world lives in our feeling. The world's existence is within it.

Now we must achieve, to the extent possible, tranquility of heart, the Guardian warns, so that we can extinguish what lives and interweaves as feeling in the dream-pictures, just as dreams are extinguished in deep sleep. Then we can reach the truth of feeling, and we can see human feeling interwoven with the cosmic life that is present in spirit in all our surroundings. And then the real spiritual human being appears to us, who in his body lives at first in his half-existence. The human being appears to us from out of sleeping feeling. We feel ourselves to be on the other side of the threshold, on the other side of the yawning abyss of being, for feeling has fallen asleep and the cosmic creative powers, which live in feeling, have appeared around us.

See in feeling's weaving in the soul,
How in sleep's dim-like dawning
Life streams in from cosmic distance;
Let in sleep through tranquil heart
Human feeling waft away hushed;
And cosmic life spiritualizes
As the human being's power.

[This second part is written on the blackboard.]

II

See in

(Before it was "behind", here it is "in"; all the words in a mantric verse are important.)

feeling's weaving in the soul,

(Before it was "thinking", here "feeling"; there "sensory light", here "weaving in the soul"; "weaving" is much more real than merely semblance of light.)

[In the first part "thinking" and "sensory light", and in the second part "feeling's" are underlined.

How in sleep's dim-like dawning
Life streams in from cosmic distance;

(There it was “Willing arises from the body's depths;”, here “Life streams in from cosmic distance;”)

[In the third line of the first part “Willing” is underlined, and in the second part “Life”.]

> *Let in sleep through tranquil heart*
> *Human feeling waft away hushed;*

It is enhanced: Here [in the first part] it involved letting flow through the soul's force; here [in the second part] one must waft away human feeling. [the word “waft” is underlined.]

> *And cosmic life spiritualizes*

— here [in the first part] it was the willing that is still in the human being; here it is cosmic

> *As the human being's power.*

— the enhancement relative to cosmic thought's creation. —

[In the first part “cosmic thought´s creation” and in the second part “human being's power” are underlined.]

The Guardian of the Threshold indicates to us that we should look back once again at the gray figure that stands over there, which we are ourselves in earthly life, but this time after having turned away, in our minds we turn it around in a circle. We will find, when we rotate the figure, that the sun appears behind it and rotates with it. [It is drawn - left, red]. And we will realize that at the moment we are brought into physical existence from the spiritual world, our etheric body has been compressed from the cosmic ether. Therefore, just as the first verse belongs to this [the drawing of the gray figure and the first verse are numbered “I”], this second verse belongs to this. [The drawing of the red rotating form and the second verse are numbered “II”.]

Then the Guardian of the Threshold refers us to our will, which is active in our limbs. And he strongly draws our attention to the fact that whatever relates to the will is in a sleeping state, even when we are awake. He explains how as the thought works downward - I explained it last time, so may say it now -, how as the thought carries warmth downward into our limbs' movement so that it becomes will: this becomes clear in spiritual cognition and spiritual seeing. Normal consciousness hides this when we are sleeping, as it hides life in general during sleep. Now we should observe the will in the limbs as though sunken in deep sleep. The will is asleep. The limbs are asleep. We should see this as a firm mental image. Then, when it is firm, we realize how thinking, the source of willing in earthly man, sinks down into the limbs. Then it becomes light in him. The will becomes bright. It wakes up. When we first see it in its sleeping state, we find that it wakes up when thinking sinks downward and light from below streams upward, which is the force of gravity. Feel the force of gravity in your legs and arms when you let them relax: that is what streams upward, and which meets with the downward streaming thinking. We observe human will transformed into its reality and thinking appearing as what ignites the will in man in an enchanting, magical way. That is the truly magical effect of thinking on the will. It is magic. Now we become aware of it. The Guardian of the Threshold says:

See above the bodily effects of will,
— in the aura —
How into sleeping fields of activity
Thinking sinks down from head forces;
Let through the soul's vision of light
human will transform itself;
And thinking, it appears
As the magical essence of will.

[This third verse, with underlining, is written on the blackboard.]

III

See above the bodily effects of will,

How into sleeping fields of activity
Thinking sinks down from head forces;
Let through the soul's vision of light
human will transform itself;
And thinking, it appears
As the magical essence of will.

Now we imagine that the Guardian of the Threshold again points to the person over there, who we are ourselves, telling us to look and retain the picture, but not to turn around, but to let this picture sink below the surface of the earth beneath where the figure is standing. We look over there. There stands the one who we ourselves are. We make the picture and develop the strong force to look below, as though a lake were there and we were looking at this image as now being within the earth, but not as a mirror-image, but as an upright figure. [Draws.]

We imagine this picture: the earth [A white arc is drawn.] belonging to the third verse [This drawing and the third verse are given the number III.] We imagine: how the earth's gravitational forces rise, how the gravitational forces illuminate the limbs, feet and arms [white arrows]. In later observation, we acquire an idea of how gods and humans cooperate between death and a new birth to arrange karma.

That is what the Guardian of the Threshold admonishes us about when he speaks to us for the first time after we have crossed over the yawning abyss of being.

See behind thinking's sensory light,
How in the gloomy spirit-cell
Willing arises from the body's depths;
Let be cast, through your strength of soul,
Dead thinking into the cosmic void;
And willing, it will arise
As cosmic thought's creation.

See in feeling's weaving in the soul,
How in sleep's dim-like dawning
Life streams in from cosmic distance;
Let in sleep through tranquil heart
Human feeling waft away hushed;
And cosmic life spiritualizes
As the human being's power.

See above the bodily effects of will,
How into sleeping fields of activity
Thinking sinks down from head forces;
Let through the soul's vision of light
human will transform itself;
And thinking, it appears
As the magical essence of will.

The circle always closes. We are looking again at the starting point, listening to all the beings and all the processes of the world:

O man, know thyself!
So resounds the Cosmic-Word.
You hear it strong in soul,
You feel it firm in spirit.

Who speaks with such cosmic might?
Who speaks with such depth of heart?

Does it work through distant radiant space
Into your senses' sense of being?
Does it ring through weaving waves of time
Into your life's evolving stream?

It's you yourself who,
In feeling space, in experiencing time,
The Word create, feeling foreign
In space's soulless void,
Because you lose the force of thought
In time's destroying flow.

By this affirmation, Michael is present in this, his rightfully existing School. His presence is confirmed by his sign, which should loom over everything given in this School:

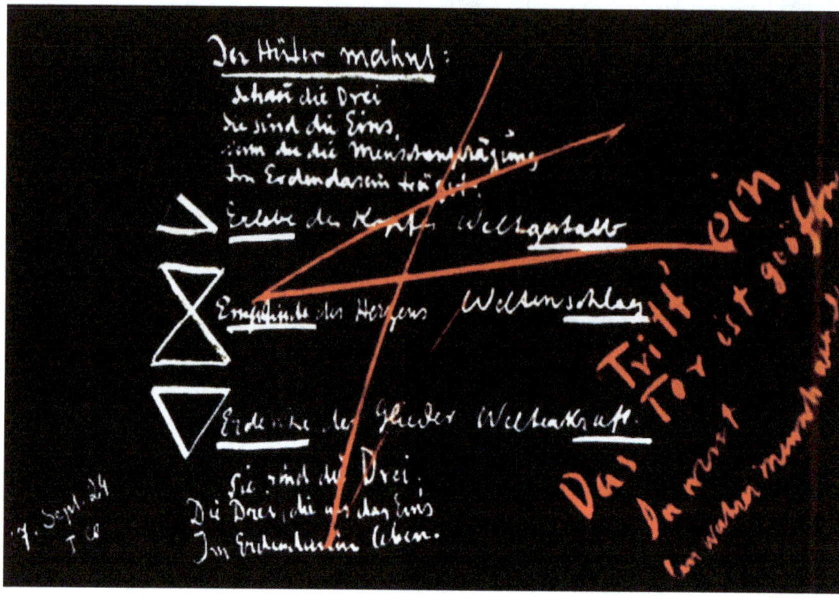

[Michael Sign - in red]

It is confirmed by his seal, that he has impressed on the esoteric striving of the Rosicrucian School, and which lives on symbolically in the threefold verse:

Ex deo nascimur

In Christo morimur

Per spiritum sanctum reviviscimus

And as Michael impresses his seal, the first sentence is spoken with this gesture:

[draws: Image 1, the lower seal gesture, yellow]

The second sentence with this gesture:

[draws: Image 1, the middle seal gesture, yellow]

The third sentence with this gesture:

[draws: Image 1, the upper seal gesture]

The first gesture means:[3]

I esteem the Father

It lives mutely as we say: "Ex deo nascimur".

[lower seal gesture]

The second gesture means:

I love the Son

It lives mutely as we say: "In Christo morimur".

[middle seal gesture]

The third gesture means:

I unite with the Spirit

It lives mutely in the Sign, which is Michael's Seal, as we speak: "Per spiritum sanctum reviviscimus".

[upper seal gesture]

Thus, today's Michael affirmation is confirmed by means of his Sign and Seals:

[Michael's Sign]

[spoken with the seal gestures:]

Ex deo nascimur

In Christo morimur

Per spiritum sanctum reviviscimus.

***

Translator's notes:

[1] It is a fairly common practice in Germany and Switzerland for people who come early to a function to place a paper, notebook, or hat on a chair to reserve their places.

[2] It seems to me, although the editors of the German original say nothing about it, that Rudolf Steiner was being ironic here, that a School member gave the mantra to his unauthorized friend, who then passed it on to others, and that the member then used the "clairvoyant" story as an excuse.

[3] The Michael Sign and Seals: From the stenographic notes of the seven recapitulation lessons, it is not possible to determine when Rudolf Steiner only wrote the words on the blackboard or when he spoke the words and wrote them, or only spoke them.

***

This was the last Lesson for the Esoteric School. Rudolf Steiner was unable to continue because of illness. He died on March 30, 1925.

Rudolf Steiner Portrait

by Peter Gospodinov

Peter Gospodinov was born in 1974. During the period, 1994 – 1997, he attended the Art Academy Sofia, BG. During the period, 1999 – 2003, he attended the Visual Art School in Basel. For more information on Peter, use this URL: https://www.petergos.com/

CPSIA information can be obtained
at www.ICGtesting.com
Printed in the USA
LVHW080747080522
718001LV00029B/304/J

9 781948 302326